(Faith, Hope and Love)

(Faith, Hope and Love)

Vol. One: In Your Eyes

JEFFREY E. POLLOCK

authorHOUSE®

AuthorHouse™
1663 Liberty Drive
Bloomington, IN 47403
www.authorhouse.com
Phone: 1-800-839-8640

Published by AuthorHouse   11/01/2012

ISBN: 978-1-4772-7920-5 (sc)
ISBN: 978-1-4772-7919-9 (e)

DEDICATION

This heart work is all for Jesus our Lord and Savior without whom true love would not exist; He is my strength and my song! For every saint in Christ Jesus who knows and shares His redeeming love with a smile in their heart! To God be the glory, praise the Lord! — Praise the Lord, praise the Lord, Let the earth hear His voice! Praise the Lord, praise the Lord, Let the people rejoice! O come to the Father, through Jesus the Son, and give Him the glory, great things He hath done! — Fanny J. Crosby

For my beautiful bride the precious wife of my youth and most cherished friend Evelyn Lynn Teal-Pollock with whom in God's amazing grace I learned to worship Jesus for who He really is, the one true God! For Evelyn's parents Robert and Shirley who I dearly loved; her beloved sisters Deborah Matteson, Elaine Lavender and Sharon Hobbs, their darling husbands and dear children with whom I've known the great joy of being uncle and brother-in-law for 20 years!

For my wonderful parents Joseph and Nanette Pollock; my brother Joe and his wife Debra and their precious daughters Nanette, Elizabeth and Madeline; my brother David and his wife Cheryl and their son Bennett; my sister Karen and her husband Hayden Clark, their son Hayden and daughter Charli; my brother Douglas and his wife Haydee and their beautiful daughter Leslie!

EVELYN

When I remember Evelyn
I remember LOVE
Never had a girl ever
Loved me like she did

I remember FAITH
The way she loved Jesus
In spite of her suffering
She only loved Him more

I remember JOY
In her lovely face
Her smile lit my heart
And filled my life with grace

I remember HOPE
The way she prayed to Jesus
Confident of His perfect love
As she spoke His name

When I remember Evelyn
I remember JESUS
I remember love
When I remember Evelyn

JEFFREY POLLOCK
JUNE 11, 2010

AARON DAVID

Ask my son for a hand,
He'd share his heart;
He was that kind of man.
Ask my brother for a prayer,
He'd share his faith;
He was that kind of man.
Reach out and touch his life,
He'd share his soul;
He was that kind of man.
Offer him a simple tear,
He'd stay until you smiled;
He was that kind of man.
Need a friend to help you stand,
He'd stay right by your side;
He was that kind of man,
Dare to judge another's heart,
His would break with sorrow;
He was that kind of man.
Ask my friend and you'll receive,
He was born to give his all;
That's the kind of man he was.
Visit him with eyes now closed,
See him embracing Heaven;
That's the kind of saint he was and is.
Indeed our Savior paid the price,
And called His beloved child Home;
God found him ready to be with Jesus!
Dance my brother, dance!

For my nephew
August 8, 2001

ISAIAH 40:31

ALWAYS AND FOREVER

High above
This valley low
The God of love
Is mine to know

Deep inside
This wounded heart
The God of life
Is my North Star

Ever wider
His awesomeness
The Living Word
Will guide my steps

Forever with me
His eternal promise
The God of peace
I am His

PSALMS 73:26

AN INNOCENT MAN

Where are they taking You, my Lord?
Teach them what You came here for!
Teach them how to pray to our Father!
Don't just give up without saying a word!

Where are they taking You, my Truth?
Talk to them about believing in You!
Talk to them about Heaven and Love!
God, don't let this happen to Jesus!

Where are they taking You, my Life?
Talk to them about walking in the light!
Talk to them about turning back to God!
Don't die like a sinner—hanging on a cross!

Where are they taking You, my King?
Tell them You haven't done anything!
Tell them You came to save them too!
Don't let this happen, God, not to You!

MARK 15:15

ISAIAH 53:7
He is brought as a lamb to the slaughter.

ANOTHER DAY

Another day my eyes will open,
To leave the night the light has broken;
Until I must lie down again to sleep,
Help me, my Lord, Your ways to keep.

This is the day my ears will hear,
The faithful call of the God I fear;
This is the day my heart will worship,
It's only Savior from death and sin.

This is the day my voice will answer,
The One I adore Who made this day;
This is the day my dreams will cease,
As I awaken to His joyful release!

This is the day my soul will rejoice,
The hope I have in Christ my Lord;
Who paid the price to set me free,
So I will love Him more than me.

Another day my eyes have opened,
To leave the night the light has broken;
Let me not lay down again to sleep,
Until my Father Your way I keep.

LAMENTATIONS 3:22-24
". . . new every morning . . ."

AT JESUS' FEET

All I can do with my life
Is lay it down at Jesus' feet;
If I say I truly love the Lord,
What more can I hope for.

All I can do with my gifts,
Is lay them at Jesus' feet;
To spend my life at Jesus' feet,
What else do I really need?

If all I accomplish with my life,
Is worship our wonderful Lord;
A successful life I'd have lead,
On my knees at Jesus' feet.

In life it doesn't matter what I do for me,
The crowns I earn aren't mine to keep;
All I can do when my life is through,
Is lay it down at Jesus' feet.

THANK YOU LORD!

ATTITUDE OF GRATITUDE

When everything seems to be going wrong
And nothing seems to come back right
I won't raise my fists in the air
And challenge Jesus to a fight

When all my skies are grey
And pain is pouring down
When tears are welling up inside
Falling heavy to the ground

When my heart is broken
Raining bloody tears
And I'm paranoid to the point
Of denying all my fears

When no one wants to be my friend
And nobody really seems to care
I won't deny the Lord is true
His help is always there

I will see the good in others
For as long as my life takes
I will glorify my God, my Savior
With a joyful heart of grateful praise

THANK YOU, LORD!
Habakkuk 3:17-18

AUTUMN LEAVES

The Sun rises somewhere
on a distant horizon of my mind
and spreads God's light over and
onto the dark side of my life,
chasing shadows and scattering
the ghosts that hide close to my heart.
The Sun exposes the rotting flesh of the
wretched man I am and burns away
the awful mask I wear to cover the
fears I nurse with the spoiled fruit
of my own will. The Son shines eternal
truth upon the barren moon of my tortured
soul, releasing power destined to change
my course and steer my ship into uncharted
waters of joy and wonder, courage and
praise. The Son burns God's love into my
being and forms in me the very likeness
of righteousness, which eventually
fills every measure of my spirit with the
same self-giving presence that typified
Christ Jesus on this earth. The Son
reaches out through me to touch other
people and, by His Spirit, brings them to
the knowledge of His grace and kindness.
The Sun sets like Autumn leaves that
live and die with the passing of time;
forever falling, forever rising
to live again.

BACK TO A FUTURE

Take your eyes off the world for a minute,
Realize how entrenched you are in it;
Now pull yourself out of the ditch you are in,
Come back to the One who freed you from sin.

Lay a foundation of love and good works,
On the Rock of Salvation, the Living Word;
Don't let the sand in your past hold you down,
When it's your time to fulfill God's purpose now.

Make up your mind to go forward from here,
Back to a future not hindered by fear;
Build your life on Christ who died on a cross,
To give you a Father and bring you to God.

Come back to the One who freed you from sin,
And let you out of the pit of death you were in;
Understand God knows you can't save yourself,
So believe in Jesus before you wind up in Hell.

Now turn your eyes back on the world for awhile,
Pray for the courage to trust God and smile;
People must know their only hope is God's Son,
So put your faith in Jesus and get the job done!

JEREMIAH 29:13
. . . search for me with all your heart."

The Spirit of the Lord GOD is upon me; because the LORD hath anointed me to preach good tidings unto the meek; he hath sent me to bind up the brokenhearted, to proclaim liberty to the captives, and the opening of the prison to them that are bound; ² To proclaim the acceptable year of the LORD, and the day of vengeance of our God; to comfort all that mourn; ³ To appoint unto them that mourn in Zion, to give unto them beauty for ashes, the oil of joy for mourning, the garment of praise for the spirit of heaviness; that they might be called trees of righteousness, the planting of the LORD, that he might be glorified.

BEAUTY FOR ASHES

My eyes
Blind from birth
Closed in darkness
No hint of light brings
Color to my damaged life
Only blackness.

My ears
Deaf to compassion
Clothed in silence
No whisper from God
Brings any hope
Only heaviness.

My hands
Dirtied in this world
Full of burned ashes
No sensations of life
Reach my fingertips
Only death.

My heart
Broken by chains
Wrapped in fear of death
No rest from religion
Conquers my anger
Only pain.

The Cross!
A flood falls from my eyes!
Spikes tear through His flesh!
Blood of Life pours from His beaten body!
The perfect Lamb breathes His last . . . and He dies!

My eyes are opened as I see Him now!
My ears hear His Voice and I fall to repent!
My hands are cleansed by His precious blood!
My broken heart beats anew with confidence as
My mind begins to understand beauty for ashes!

The Lord is my light and my salvation; whom shall I fear?
The Lord is the strength of my life; of whom shall I be afraid?

BECAUSE I LOVE YOU

Because I love You
I trust the words You say
I believe You guard my way
I worship You in spirit and truth
I train my heart to want to pray
I turn my eyes away from sin
Because I love You

Because I love You
I watch for Your return
I use each day I live to learn
I praise You for making me new
I conform my will to Your Word
I run the race I'm in to win
Because I love You

Because I love You
I ask Your Spirit to guide my steps
I seek Your peace and righteousness
I knock on Your door 'til I get through
I humble my soul to honor me less
I hope to glorify You while I live
Because I love You

BEHOLD

Behold the Babe,
Born in a feeding trough;
Come to light the holy way,
Cradled by a mother's love,

Behold the Boy,
Teaching in the synagogue;
Who with competent voice,
Taught the mysteries of God.

Behold the Man,
Baptized in the Jordan;
Witness to our Father's plan,
To give everlasting joy to man.

Behold the Lamb,
Our sinless sacrifice;
Lift your eyes to see I AM,
And behold the risen Christ.

MATTHEW 1:23
*Behold, a virgin shall be with child, and shall bring forth a son, and
they shall call his name Emmanuel, which being interpreted is,
God with us.*

BEYOND AND ABOVE

Our Father is for us!
Who can be against us?
He did not spare His Son.
Nothing more need be done!

All of God has been given to us,
To provide for us the Way to Heaven.
God has shown us the Light of His Love,
To reveal the Truth of what's beyond and above.

Christ Jesus came to earth to live a Carpenter's life,
And built by His example the true purpose for our lives.
Although the world always fights against the Hope in me,
It can't argue with Almighty God the awesome fact I'm free!

ROMANS 8:31-33

BLIND

Groping through blackness . . .
Searching for anything . . .
Falling, finding no peace.

Stumbling in darkness . . .
Praying for understanding . . .
Calling, seeing no light.

Wandering in confusion . . .
Feeling God's touch,
Turning, then coming home.

LIGHT

Trusting Jesus,
Following in freedom,
Worshiping, knowing Love!

Resting in God's promises,
Standing up for integrity;
Giving, receiving Joy!

Walking in brilliance!
Wanting for nothing!
Living, enjoying Life!

JOHN 8:12

BLOOD FELL

Blood fell
And washed me clean

Blood fell
And set my spirit free

Blood fell
And purified my heart

Blood fell
And wiped away scars

Blood fell
And opened blind eyes

Blood fell
And left me justified

Blood fell
And healed me as I was falling

His blood fell on me
And cleansed me from all sin

Thank You Jesus!

BORN AGAIN

No true freedom outside the light of our Lord,
Liberty is witness of what Jesus died for;
Family and friendships, celebration and fellowship,
Purpose for living is to praise Jesus more!

No true choices without the light of our Lord,
Hope today depends on Who we choose to live for;
Honor and worship, obedience and discipline,
Quality of life comes from the Holy Spirit's store.

No healthy fruit outside the light of our Lord,
Joy today is in doing what Jesus did and more;
Praying and helping, encouraging and healing,
Empowered through Christ to win every war.

No true faith without the light of Christ our Lord,
Through Jesus' love we are more than conquerors;
Grace and compassion, mercy and forgiveness,
Reason for living is to practice Holy Scriptures.

No true love outside the light of Jesus Christ our Lord,
In His power and by His grace again we are born;
Growing and changing, hoping and praising,
We know our God is sovereign over every storm.

No true life without freedom found in Jesus,
He is the Living Lord of the universe!
He is the Only Way to reach our Father.
He is the Truth who frees us!

ROMANS 8:37

CALL HIS NAME JESUS

Call out His name when you cannot see,
Reach for His hand and find God's mercy.
Call the name JESUS when you can't stand,
Lean on His strength to obey His commands.

Call on His name when you come to The Cross,
Fall at His feet and know the love of God.
Call His name JESUS when you choose to submit,
Depend upon His grace to rise again and live.

You shall call His name JESUS, for He will save
His people from their sins.—Matthew 1:21, NKJV

PSALM 118:24
This is the day the LORD has made;
Let us rejoice and be glad in it.

CELEBRATE LIFE

This is the day the Lord has made,
Perfected in glory by His sovereign strength;
Let us choose even now to make a joyful noise,
Loving God in purity as we live and rejoice!

Today is branded new by God's redeeming grace,
Washed clean of the sin we spent lost time in;
Every morning is created with love that is true,
For saints who by faith are waiting for the Lord.

Each day made afresh,
Resplendent with mercy from heaven,
Breaks through the night with new light,
Joyfully compelling us to celebrate life!

1 Corinthians 5:8

CHOICE TO MAKE

A cross I can't put down,
I also have a choice to make;
There is a cost that I must count,
If I'm going to live for Jesus' sake.

Jesus' Name is on the line,
When I step out in faith to live;
The course I take is direct and concise,
I will walk in truth and avoid all sin.

I have a mission and I have a goal,
I also have a choice to make;
There are rules that I must follow,
If I'm going to prosper under God's grace.

I will walk in truth and avoid all sin,
The course I'll take is direct and concise;
When I step out in faith to live,
and Jesus' Name is on the line.

If I'm going to live for Jesus' sake,
There is a cost that I must count;
I also have a choice to make,
A cross I can't put down.

LUKE 14:25-27

CHOSEN

Before time began
In the very mind of God,
Our Father had a plan
To teach us how to love.

Naked at our birth
We came to life in blood,
And fought for air on earth
Under the watch-care of God.

Chosen before time
In the very heart of God,
Our Savior knew He had to die
To give us new birth at the Cross.

Now dressed in His own righteousness
We walk by faith the way Christ taught,
And claim His victory over sin and death
As we encourage each other to worship God.

COLOSSIANS 3:12-13

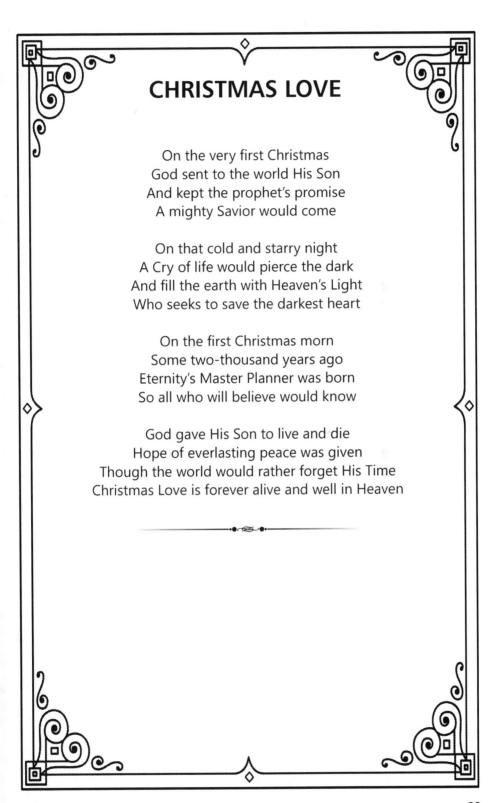

CHRISTMAS LOVE

On the very first Christmas
God sent to the world His Son
And kept the prophet's promise
A mighty Savior would come

On that cold and starry night
A Cry of life would pierce the dark
And fill the earth with Heaven's Light
Who seeks to save the darkest heart

On the first Christmas morn
Some two-thousand years ago
Eternity's Master Planner was born
So all who will believe would know

God gave His Son to live and die
Hope of everlasting peace was given
Though the world would rather forget His Time
Christmas Love is forever alive and well in Heaven

*If the blind put their hand in God's they find
their way more surely than those who see but
have not faith or purpose.—Helen Keller*

CLOSE YOUR EYES

Close your eyes and see
See your world in the dark
Dark and blue sky come together
Together as clouds in midnight dreams

Dreams tell their own stories
Stories so full of anxiety and joy
Joy and worry paint fading pictures
Pictures made with watercolors in the rain

Rain falls against sealed windows
Windows shut tight against raging storms
Storms of life: storms of anger, storms of sorrow
Sorrow as bloody tears flooding the eyes of Christ

Christ and Christ alone opens our hearts
Hearts with eyes closed in fear of what will get in
For sorrow He gives joy; for anger, sovereign grace
Grace quenches fury and holds sainted sinners close

EPHESIANS 1

CLOUDS

One day Lord I'll meet You in the clouds
Today Jesus you make my life worth living

Soon my King I will bow before Your throne
Help me bow even now before I get to Heaven

One day my Shepherd I'll follow You on streets of gold
Today Lord Jesus your Way is what I want to learn

Soon my Master I'll hear You in the clouds
Help me even now to be obedient to Your Word

One day my Love I'll see you face to face
Today my Light help me love this human race

Soon, my Savior, I'll know the Truth beyond all doubts
Help me now to know You before I meet you in the clouds

1 THESSALONIANS 4:13-18

And so we will be with the Lord forever.
Therefore encourage each other with these words.

COLOR ME GRACE

MERCY
WAKE ME
CHANGE ME
WASH ME

DRAW ME
CATCH ME
COVER ME
CRUSH ME

BREAK ME
BAPTIZE ME
CONVINCE ME
CLOTHE ME

FIND ME
HOLD ME
FORGIVE ME
HEAL ME

INVADE ME
SEARCH ME
FINISH ME
SEND ME

CALL ME
ENCOURAGE ME
COLOR ME
GRACE

COME TO JESUS

Come to Jesus
Sent from above
Come to Jesus
Fear not His love

Come to Jesus
Lay your burdens down
Come to Jesus
Rejoice in the sound

Come to Jesus
Trust in Him today
Come to Jesus
Be healed by faith

Come to Jesus
Take on His yoke
Come to Jesus
Find peace and hope

MATTHEW 11:28-30

COME TO THE CROSS

The Light of the World
Shines hope on the lost;
Look closely at the Lord,
And come to the Cross.

The Shepherd of the World
Cries out to find the lost;
Live closely to the Lord,
And come to the Cross.

The Savior of the World,
Tells truth for the lost;
Listen closely to the Lord,
And come to the Cross.

The Sovereign of the universe,
Sent His Son to save the Earth;
Learn from Jesus—stay close to God,
And come now be saved at the Cross.

COURAGEOUS

Step out in FAITH
On new years day
Walk in TRUTH
That will not change

Step up to LOVE
That came from above
Walk in NEW LIFE
Trusting in the Lord Jesus

Step up to HEAVEN
In Two-thousand-Twelve
Walk in PEACE
Where all things work well

Step out in FAITH
Each and every new day
Walk in the STRENGTH
That never fades

AMEN

COME

Come to the Cross
The Cross of Forgiveness

Come to the Cross
The End of the Line

Come to the Cross
The Cross of Redemption
Come meet the God of your life

Come to the Cross
The Cross of Completion

Come to the Cross
the Start of New Life

Come to the Cross
The Cross of Conviction
Come lay your life on the line

Come to the Cross
Be reconciled to God

Jesus gave Himself to be your Savior
COME MEET GOD AT THE CROSS

Create in me a clean heart, O God;
and renew a right spirit within me.

CREATE IN ME A CLEAN HEART

Wash me God, make me clean;
Fill me God, make me wise.

Hold me Lord, keep me still;
Break me Lord, mold my will.

Wash me God, make me pure;
Teach me God, make me real.

Fill me Lord, make me whole;
Love me Lord, fill my soul.

Wash me God, make me clean;
Change me God, make me holy.

Lead me Lord, make me humble;
Catch me Lord, when I stumble.

Touch me Lord, I will see;
Wash me God, I will be clean.

Teach me Jesus, I will discern;
Touch me Jesus and I will learn.

Give me light, Father, I will shine;
Give me Yourself, You will be mine.

Wash me, and I shall be whiter than snow.

PSALM 51:7B

THANK YOU LORD!

Looking unto Jesus the author and finisher of our faith; who for the joy that was set before him endured the cross, despising the shame, and is set down at the right hand of the throne of God.

CROSS YOUR HEART

Does joy cross your mind,
When sin leaves you blind;
Does Jesus help you see,
How the truth sets you free?

Does joy cross your heart,
When pain won't depart;
Does Jesus help you cope,
When friends run low on hope?

Does joy cross your soul,
When despair takes its toll;
Does Jesus help you out,
When you fall into doubt?

Do you rejoice in the Cross,
When you pause to think of God;
Do you cling with all your strength,
To the Savior whom Our Father sent?

CRY

On a night so high and holy,
Stars sang out with light galore;
As heaven lead the shepherds solely,
To the place where Christ was born.

In a stable low and earthy,
The Messiah made his humble entrance;
As angels wondered at the sight,
The baby Jesus begins to cry.

Cry sweet baby, cry for life,
Cry for hunger, cry for light;
Cry sweet baby, cry for us,
Who refuse to cry for Jesus.

In a heart so lost and lonely,
The Lord makes his majestic entrance;
And angels celebrate at the sight,
As a baby Christian begins to cry.

LUKE 2:8-14

And he said to them all, If any man will come after me,
let him deny himself, and take up his cross daily,
and follow me. LUKE 9:23

DAILY CROSS

Every day my heart beat sounds,
I wake to hear my Lord's true call;
Follow me and bear my wounds,
In faith and love, be straight and tall.

Painful cries each day will bring
a closer walk to Christ's commands;
Love one another as I loved you,
Build your lives on rock not sand.

Prayerful sighs each breath will take
a further route to reach God's ear;
Dancing closer to the burning flame,
Deny thyself your haunting fear.

Every day my heartbeat sounds,
A deeper love within my chest;
The cross I bear I'll soon lay down,
At Jesus' feet I'll surely rest.

But for now my love I'll bear the wait,
The Weight was borne by Christ alone;
I believe my Lord will soon return,
Until that day I'll follow Him home.

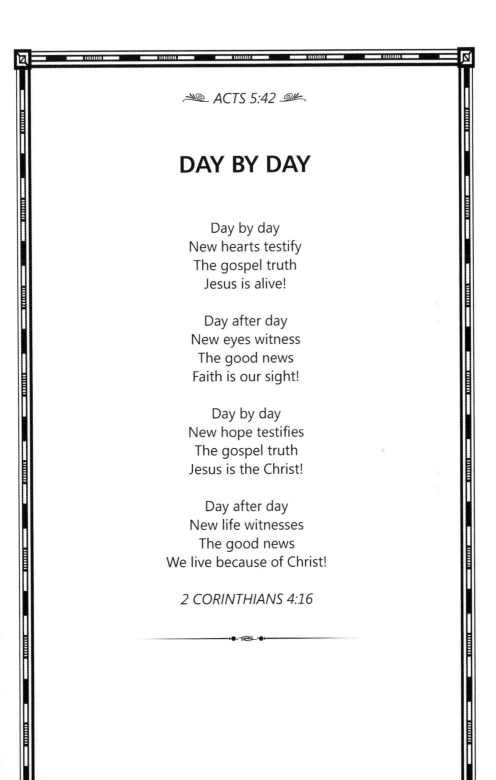

≈ ACTS 5:42 ≈

DAY BY DAY

Day by day
New hearts testify
The gospel truth
Jesus is alive!

Day after day
New eyes witness
The good news
Faith is our sight!

Day by day
New hope testifies
The gospel truth
Jesus is the Christ!

Day after day
New life witnesses
The good news
We live because of Christ!

2 CORINTHIANS 4:16

DAY IN DAY OUT

Day in day out
The Sun shines
Upon our faces.

Night falls God calls
The Father shines
Upon our souls.

Sun rise Son sent
The Son shines
Upon our hearts.

Jesus came Christ went
The Holy Spirit shines
Upon our minds

Day in day out
His Light shines
Upon our lives!

ENJOY!

Life is short
Enjoy the moment
But keep your focus
On the Lord

Time is fleeting
So revel in freedom
Enjoy your life
But remember Jesus

Remember Jesus
Who paid the price
To conquer sin and death
And open blind eyes

Thank God for your life
Sing praises to Heaven
And while you're at it
Enjoy every second

PSALMS 100:4

"Rejoice in the Lord always: and again I say, rejoice"

ENJOY YOUR LIFE

All the day is glorious,
All the day is holy;
All the day is made for us,
To praise God in His glory.

All the day is perfect,
All the day is blessed;
All the day is beautiful,
Sunrise and sunset.

All the day is love,
All the day is grace;
Be glad—enjoy life,
Each and every day!

ETERNAL HOPE

Immured within
These black walls of sin
Condemned by conscience
Darkness rules my senses

Trapped inside
These halls of time
Confounded by evil
Fear controls my will

Pressured from without
The walls fell down
Enlightened by Truth
God's grace made me new

Freed from the inside out
Cleansed from haunting doubt
Befriended by ALMIGHTY God
Eternal Hope is mine at the Cross!

1 JOHN 2:2

FOCUS ON HEAVEN

The way of God is a costly thing
We are revived in Christ's very dying
The Cross of Jesus bought our hope
And changes the way we think of sin

The truth of God is a holy thing
We are renewed through Christ's bodily rising
The Power of Jesus strengthens our hope
And changes the way we choose to live

The life of God is a precious thing
We are reborn in Christ's very living
The Presence of Jesus is our hope
Changing the way we see everything

The will of God is a perfect thing
We are saved by grace through faith in redemption
The resurrection of our Lord Jesus Christ is hope
That sharpens our focus on heaven

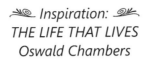

⁓ Inspiration: ⁓
THE LIFE THAT LIVES
Oswald Chambers

ETERNITY NOW

Take your focus off the past,
Refuse to worry for the future;

Each and every day you live,
Awake in search of treasure;

Store up all the truth you find,
Until your heart overflows;

Rest and know eternity now,
Endless peace will follow.

EVERY MOMENT

For every sight the eyes could see,
For every thought a mind can think,
For every joy and pain the heart may know,
I praise You Lord with all my soul!

For every holy gift a spirit receives,
For every Sovereign lift You've given me,
For all the peace and sorrow my heart has known,
I praise You Lord my God with all my soul!

For every grace a man might need,
For every time I have prayed for mercy,
For every fitted piece of spiritual armor,
With my heart and soul I praise You Lord!

For every moment of my life,
For every beat You grant this heart,
For all Your love poured out on the Cross,
For my eternal soul I praise You Lord my God!

PRAISE JESUS!!!

EVERY THOUGHT PEACE

God, grant me a joyful song
A simple poem of trust and perseverance
Give me Your mercy new
In conscious hope holiness

God, grant me a righteous fear
Solemn awe and reverence
Give me Your presence near
In conscious light goodness

God, grant me a patient heart
Quiet grace and confidence
Give me Your power strong
In conscious peace rest

God, grant me a perfect aim
Sincere faith and obedience
Give me Your wisdom true
In conscious thought protection

2 CORINTHIANS 10:4-6
ISAIAH 26:3

EVERYTHING I NEED

With heart in hand I come
Lord God to take You at Your Word;
With the knowledge of Your mercy
I am cleansed through Jesus' blood,
And bow before You God my Father.

With hope in Christ I stand
Lord God before You with this prayer;
With peace beyond my understanding
I bravely choose to give my love to You,
And trust your love for me is just and fair.

With faith in Jesus I still tremble
Lord God before Your throne of grace;
Within myself I find the courage You give
To enter the holy courts of Your compassion,
And humbly fall in reverence to my face.

With joy in Jesus Christ my Lord
God my tears fall down upon Your feet;
As my cheek touches the scars
That bid welcome to Eternal Paradise,
I am reminded You are everything I need.

EPHESIANS 3:12

EVERYTHING TO ME

You are my life.
You are my love.
You are my Lord.
You are everything to me.

You are my light.
You are my strength.
You are my Lord.
You are everything to me.

Jesus, You're my hope.
Jesus, You're my joy.
Jesus, You're my God.
You're everything to me.

Jesus, You're my peace.
Jesus, You're my righteousness.
Jesus, You're my truth.
You are everything to me!

FACE TO FACE

Face to Face with God our Father,
My joy is COMPLETE in Him;
Head to Head with my Creator,
My mind is RENEWED in Him.

Face to Face with Christ the Lord,
My joy is made WHOLE in Him;
Heart to Heart with my Savior,
My heart is WASHED FREE of sin.

Face to Face with the Holy Spirit,
My joy is made FULL in Him;
Glory unto Glory in holiness,
My soul is REFRESHED as I sing.

Face to Face with Almighty God,
My joy is eternally NEW in Him;
Grace upon Grace at the Cross;
His love is EVERLASTING, Amen.

> < > *1 CORINTHIANS 13:12* < > <

We all, with
open face beholding
as in
a glass the glory
of the
Lord, are
changed into
the same image
from
glory to glory, even as
by
the Spirit
of the Lord.
~2 Corinthians 3:18~

FAITH

Father God
Again
I give my life
To You
Hold me close

> < > 2 CORINTHIANS 4:7-10 < > <

HEBREWS 12:1

FAITHFUL

In this race we run for Jesus
Who was victorious in LOVE
We are encouraged to be faithful
In the hope of our salvation

In the way we live for Jesus
Who is our Shepherd and LORD
We are instructed to be faithful
As we seek to be of one accord

In the work we do for Jesus
Who was obedient in His LIFE
We are commanded to be faithful
As we follow our Lord Jesus Christ

In the world we live for Jesus
Who is our Savior and LIGHT
We are reminded to be faithful
On this journey of eternal life

FAITHFUL

First and foremost all my future is in Jesus
And His forgiveness for my unfaithfulness,
I am always forever grateful for His mercy
Toward undeserving rebel-sinners like me,
He has rescued me out of a dead life of sin
For His own purpose and plan of salvation,
Unable to save myself I repent of my pride
Leaning full on new management in Christ!

GALATIANS 2:20
The life which I now live in the flesh I live by the faith.

FAITHFUL FRIENDS

For all my faithful friends,
Who trust life never ends;
This prayer is for you:
Wherever you are,
I pray you hope in Jesus.

To all my faithful friends,
Who stand up against the world;
This prayer is for you:
Whatever you do,
I pray you shine for Jesus.

For all my faithful friends,
Who know all things are new in Christ;
This prayer is for you:
Whoever you are,
I pray you depend on Jesus.

To all my faithful friends,
Who long to be with God in Heaven;
This prayer is for you:
Whenever you do,
I pray your heart finds peace in Jesus.

1 JOHN 2:2

FOCUS ON HEAVEN

The way of God is a costly thing,
We are revived in Christ's very dying;
The blood of Jesus bought our hope,
And changes the way we think of sin.

The truth of God is a holy thing,
We are renewed through Christ's bodily rising;
The power of Jesus strengthens our hope,
And changes the way we choose to live.

The life of God is a precious thing,
We are reborn in Christ's very living;
The presence of Jesus is our hope,
Changing the way we see everything.

The will of God is a perfect thing,
We are saved by grace through faith in redemption;
The resurrection of our Lord Jesus Christ is hope,
That sharpens our focus on heaven.

EPHESIANS 1:7-8

FOLLOW THE LEADER

Don't be afraid to step out in love,
And lift the Name of Jesus higher;
Be strong, be courageous, be tender, be tough,
As you walk in The Truth against the Liar.

Don't be afraid to believe there is hope,
As you lift the Name of Jesus higher;
Be joyful, be courteous, be obedient, be kind,
As you stand against the giants of your time.

Don't be afraid to speak up for purity,
And lift up Jesus' Name higher still;
Be steadfast, be devoted, be brave, be free,
As you fight the good fight of free will.

Don't be afraid to defend the truth,
And lift the Name of Jesus higher;
Be humble, be holy, be honest, be true,
As you talk of love a midst hell's fire.

Don't be afraid as you enter the battle,
And lift Jesus' Name within your own history;
Be strong, be courageous, be fruitful, be well,
As you follow Christ in His victory!

"So be strong and courageous!"
JOSHUA 1

JOSHUA 24:15
"As for me and my house, we will serve the LORD."

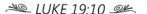

LUKE 19:10

"For the Son of Man came to seek and to save what was lost."

FOR THE LOST

The brutal scars of Crucifixion
Christ suffered in His body for you
Are imprinted on the Hands and Feet
Of the Lord of Life and Truth

The precious Blood of our Savior
Jesus shed on the Cross for you
Can set you free from sin and death
And make your old heart new

The stinging tears of Compassion
Christ wept on the Cross for you
Unite with the cries of devoted saints
Praying that you will be found soon

The Spirit of our Sovereign Lord
Jesus poured out for you at the Cross
Is the sufficient answer to God's promise
To always seek and save the lost

FOR THE PRIZE

One at a time
We start this race
On the same starting line
We receive God's grace

Won by Christ
We choose His reward
We follow our Prize
And crown Him Lord

Throughout our lives
We seek the Savior's face
Reaching for His smile
We break the final tape

We lay our lives at Jesus' feet
And one at a time we bow the knee
We finish this race the way we began
Saved by grace in God's sovereign hand

1 CORINTHIANS 9:24-27

FOREVER LOVE

Face to face with my Abba,
My joy is complete in Him;
Head to head with my Father,
My mind is renewed in Him.

Face to face with my Lord,
My joy is made whole in Him;
Hand in hand with my Savior,
I stand by His side free of sin.

Face to face with God's Spirit,
My joy is eternal in Him;
Heart to heart with my Comforter,
My soul is refreshed as I sing.

Face to face with my God,
My joy is fulfilled in Him;
Healed for eternity at the Cross;
In love that lasts forever. AMEN!

1 CORINTHIANS 13:8-13

FOREVERMORE

I love You Lord
Forevermore
I love You Lord
I love Your Word

I love You Jesus
In You I trust
I love You Lord Jesus
You loved me first

I love You Jesus
I praise You Lord
I worship You now
And forevermore

1 JOHN 4:10

FORTRESS OF FAITH

When the enemy roars
And hope fades away
Insist on standing
True in faith

When worries worsen
And darkness prevails
Instruct your heart
To be courageous

Remember God's love
When times are darkest
And press on by faith
Into His perfect rest

Stand up for Jesus
Let peace put a smile on your face
Do not be afraid what the world does
Overcome fear with mercy and grace

PROVERBS 18:10

PHILIPPIANS 3:13
I am focusing all my energies on this one thing:
Forgetting the past and looking forward to what lies ahead.

FORWARD FAITH

Look ahead and see your Father
Waiting for YOU with open arms
And as the end comes ever closer
Trust He UNDERSTANDS your heart

Focusing forward not behind you
As you work your OWN salvation out
Found in faith God's Word is truth
That leads THE WAY OUT of doubt

Pressing onward into Christ the Lord
As we learn what God's HEART is about
Stand in faith God's Word is a sword
That knows HOW TO CUT the evil out

Marching forward one day at a time
As we LIVE and LEARN that God is LOVE
Grown in faith God's Word is pure light
Pointing lost souls TO THE CROSS of Jesus

In one direction faith moves forward
As we choose to give ALL glory to God
Alive in faith we join countless others
Waiting to SEE THE FACE of God

ROMANS 5:1-2

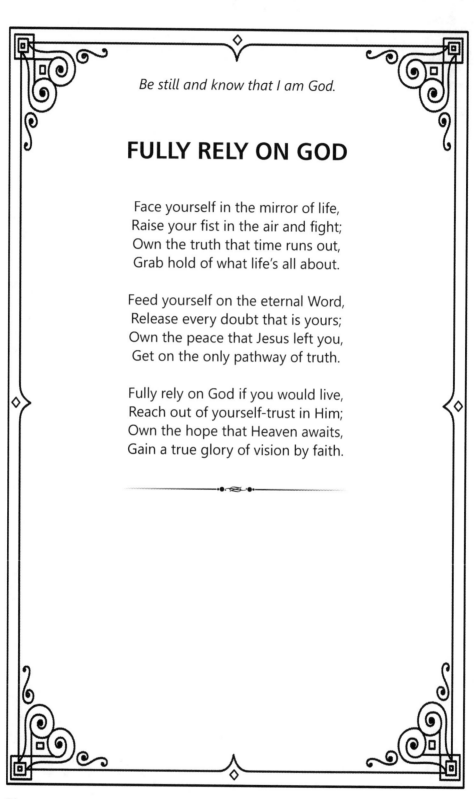

Be still and know that I am God.

FULLY RELY ON GOD

Face yourself in the mirror of life,
Raise your fist in the air and fight;
Own the truth that time runs out,
Grab hold of what life's all about.

Feed yourself on the eternal Word,
Release every doubt that is yours;
Own the peace that Jesus left you,
Get on the only pathway of truth.

Fully rely on God if you would live,
Reach out of yourself-trust in Him;
Own the hope that Heaven awaits,
Gain a true glory of vision by faith.

Today if you're feeling overwhelmed,
remember God's love and thank Him.

FREE

God came to save,
To save rebels like me;
Rebels who wanted to die,
He died to save and set free.

Freedom to have His joy,
Freedom to know His love,
Freedom to follow His way,
Freedom to believe His Son.

God came to redeem,
To redeem sinners like me;
Sinners like me who'd lost their way,
He found and gave the desire to be free.

And this be our motto: "In God is our trust."
And the star-spangled banner in triumph
shall wave O'er the land of the free
and the home of the brave!

FREEDOM

Freedom
takes
courage!
Red White and Blue
Enduring prayerfulness Enveloped
by the Truth—Dancing before God
out of love
not routine
or fear—
Man is
free only
when Christ
is revered!

07/04/08

"Freedom prospers when religion is vibrant and
the rule of law under God is acknowledged."
—Ronald Reagan

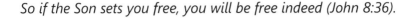

So if the Son sets you free, you will be free indeed (John 8:36).

FREED TO FLY

Freed to fly! Yes we are!
Free to fly, but when will we start?

Freed to help. Freed to serve.
Freed to help, but do we have the Gospel nerve?

Freed to speak. Freed to yell!
Freed to cry, but do we care enough to tell?

Freed to change. Freed to be transformed.
Freed to have faith, but do we really want to rise above the norm?

Freed to share. Freed to talk.
Freed to have fellowship, but will you walk like Jesus walked?

Freed to give. Freed to sow.
Freed to plant seeds of truth, but are are able to let go?

Freed to live. Freed to die to our flesh.
Freed to truly live, but will we accept Christ's victory over death?

Freed to surrender. Freed to repent of our sin.
Freed to win, but will we not return to where we've been?

Free to fly! Free to sing!
Free to worship God with all our hearts!

Freed to fly! Freed to soar!
When will we start?

FREEDOM IN JESUS

Walk in God's Light,
Hold your heart to His Way;
Live in God's Truth,
Take every chance to pray.

Trust in Eternal Life,
Put your faith in God's Love;
Stay in God's Word,
Find your freedom in Jesus!

GALATIANS 5:1
07/04/09

FREEDOM'S TOUCH

(Taste Of Eternity)

The hand of God reached down and
Turned my eyes toward the Cross of JESUS;
The BLOOD of my Lord and Savior
Fell upon this broken heart and
Healed this foolish clown.

The Light of heaven broke through
And changed my living hell to blessed hope;
The grace of God's redeeming love
Held this shattered spirit and made my life brand new!

The purpose for which I was born
Finally woke up within me;
Brushed aside my sleepy dreams,
And gave me a taste of eternity!!

The eternal wake of Christ's resurrection
Washed over me and made me clean;
Flooded my spirit, washed away my sin,
Opened my eyes and set me FREE!!!

EPHESIANS 3:16

FROM ABOVE

FROM THE TREASURE CHEST OF HEAVENLY GIFTS
POWER IS YOURS IF YOU ARE HIS;
FROM THE HOARY CONSCIENCE OF ETERNAL MIND
WISDOM IS YOURS OF A SPIRITUAL KIND;
FROM THE CONSCIOUS HEART OF ETERNITY PAST
THE STRENGTH AND LOVE OF GOD BELONGS
TO EVERYONE WHO ASKS.

JAMES 1:17

FROM GOD TO YOU

I've learned I don't have the patience
To put up with sinners like Jesus did,
But now that His Holy Spirit is in me
I have the power of His promise.

Everything I do and all I think and say
Is covered by the blood of Jesus Christ;
And now that I am baptized in His death
I'm able to stand up and live a holy life.

The fruit of holiness is not about us,
It doesn't depend on what we do;
The righteousness we have inside
Is a gift of grace from God to you.

I have a hard time with holiness,
It never came naturally to me;
But now that I'm a child of God,
Truth of Christ has set me free!

FUTURE GRACE

Don't give up,
Keep moving forward;
Fight the good fight,
Of faith in your Lord.

Don't fall down again,
Keep catching yourself;
Lift your heart to Heaven,
As a holy act of worship.

Don't stop getting up,
Keep aiming for the prize;
Press on to take firm hold,
Of future grace of Christ.

Don't trust your pride,
Keep saying faithful prayers;
Life is always an upward battle,
For those who obey and follow Jesus.

GALATIANS 6:9

GET THE WORD OUT

In Christ, the Word of God,
Rest for the weary is given;
In Christ, in Christ alone,
Faith leads to a Father in Heaven.
In Christ, in Christ alone,
Strength for the journey is found;
In Christ, in Jesus' love,
Grace becomes the sweetest sound.
The Word, the Word of God,
Cuts like the sharpest sword;
The Cross, the old rugged cross,
Sealed the faith of our Lord.
In Christ, the Word of God,
Truth lives to conquer doubt;
In Christ, in Christ alone,
Is the power to get the word out.

< < JEREMIAH 20:9 > >

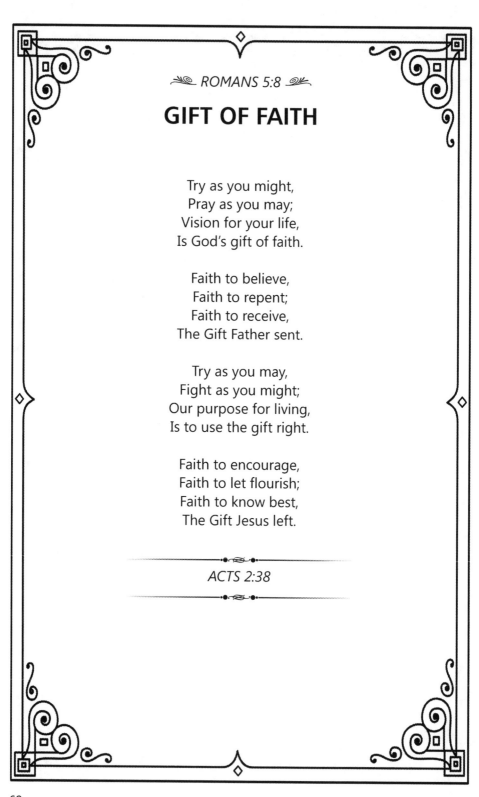

≈ ROMANS 5:8 ≈

GIFT OF FAITH

Try as you might,
Pray as you may;
Vision for your life,
Is God's gift of faith.

Faith to believe,
Faith to repent;
Faith to receive,
The Gift Father sent.

Try as you may,
Fight as you might;
Our purpose for living,
Is to use the gift right.

Faith to encourage,
Faith to let flourish;
Faith to know best,
The Gift Jesus left.

ACTS 2:38

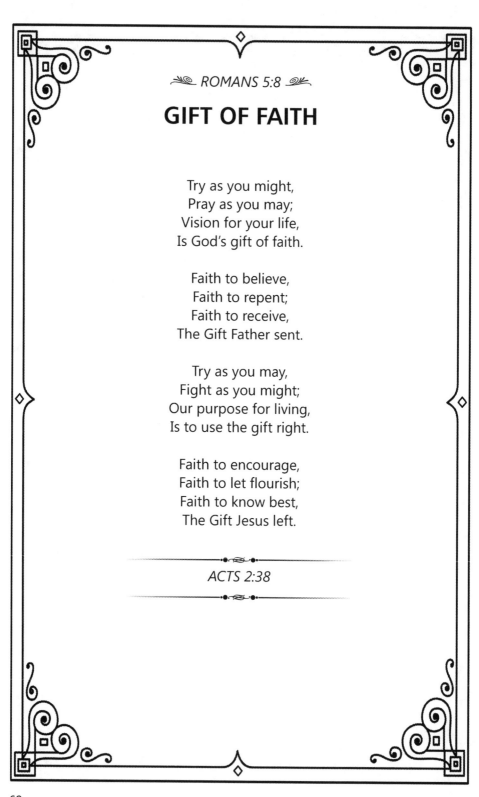

GLORY BEYOND TIME

The Source of my strength, my hope, my joy,
Is found in the cross of my Savior, my Lord;
Much higher than a mountain built over time,
Every bit of my faith is by His name not mine.

The Heart of my conscience, my peace, my love,
Is found in the center of my Redeemer, my Jesus;
Much deeper than the ocean surrounding the lands,
Every ounce of my faith is in His hands not mans.

The Purpose of my life, my vision, my surrender,
Is found in the call of my Creator, my Shepherd;
More dependable than bright stars in the sky,
Each word of my faith will live forever not die.

The Soul of my encouragement, my light, my gifts,
Is found in the company of my Creator, my King;
Much more than the imagination of man can find,
Each work of my faith is for His glory beyond time.

If my people, which are called by my name, shall humble themselves, and pray, and seek my face, and turn from their wicked ways; then will I hear from heaven, and will forgive their sin, and will heal their land.

GOD BLESS THE USA

Morning prayer
Begins another day
Reaching up to Heaven
From this world of decay

With freedom on the line
Hope leaves these lips of mine
And finds the ears of God
Listening

God help the USA
God help us see the error of our ways
God help us turn back to You today
God bless the USA

Every heartbeat
Is proof of God's eternal love
Watching over His creation
From someplace up above

With soldiers on the front line
Help us remember the providence of God
And that even during times of war
God is sovereign

God help the USA
God help us see the error of our ways
God help us all turn back to You today
God bless the USA

* * *

GOD

God is truth, God is love,
God is holy, God is light;
Christ is always on our side,
He is the very source of life.

God is perfect, God is powerful,
He is solely responsible for our lives;
Jesus Christ is worthy of our praise,
He alone is precious in our sight.

God is faithful, God is glorious,
He is peace when pressures start to rise;
Jesus Christ is worthy of our faith,
His hand will lead us through the night.

God is bigger, God is greater,
He is far above our changing times;
Christ is worthy of our worship,
He is forever esteemed in our eyes!

God is my help; the Lord
is the one who sustains me.
PSALM 54:4

God is our refuge.
PSALM 62:8

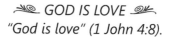
JESUS LOVES YOU

Love the Lord your God with all of your heart,
Your heart is alive and believing when you do;
When you do what you know is right you will be,
You will be in tune with the God who made you.

Love the Lord your God with all of your heart,
Your heart is at peace and behaving when you do;
When you do what you know is true you will see,
You will stay in step with God who is The Truth.

Love the Lord your God with all of your heart,
Your heart is healthily beating when you do;
When you do what you know is good you will feel,
You will feel the strength of God lifting you.

Love the Lord your God with all of your heart,
Your heart will not be benighted when you do;
When you do what God tells you, you will love life,
You will love life for in Christ all things are new!

Love the Lord your God with all of your heart,
Your heart is perfect and believing when you do;
When you do you will be right where you should be,
Believing God is love and knowing Jesus loves you.

Keep yourselves in God's love.
Jude 1:21

2 THESSALONIANS 3:5
*The Lord direct your hearts into the love of God and into the patient
waiting for Christ.*

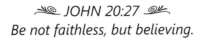

Be not faithless, but believing.

GOD OF MY FAITH

Father give me wisdom,
I pray in Jesus Name;
For a heart to know Your Son,
The Author and Finisher of faith.

Father, give me joy and grace,
I pray in Jesus Name;
For a heart to share Your Son,
The Resurrection and Life of faith.

Father give me discernment,
I pray in Jesus Name;
For a heart to love Your Son,
The Shepherd and Lamb of faith.

Father give me courage,
I pray in Jesus Name;
For a heart to obey Your Son,
The King and Master of faith.

Father grant me peace
I pray in Jesus Name;
For a heart to follow Your Son,
The Lord and God of my Faith.

"Blessed are they that have not seen, and yet have believed."
JOHN 20:29

∼ LUKE 2:10 ∼
Do not be afraid, I bring you good news.
LUKE 2:14
Glory to God in the highest, and on earth peace, good will toward men.

GOOD NEWS!

Long ago an angel spoke,
To certain shepherds in a field;
All that the prophets wrote,
Will be given to those who yield.

A Baby wrapped in rags,
Will be lying in a wooden trough;
The Living Word has come to man,
To show us how to worship God.

Long ago on a wooden cross,
A Man was crucified for all our sin;
The Living Word and Sovereign God,
Has become The Way of our redemption.

Eternity's treasure, our Father's Son,
Was sent to bring the world His Light;
Every promise of life God has given,
Is answered in the Lord Jesus Christ.

"Let us go to Bethlehem . . ."

LUKE 2:15-20

GRACE (REASON FOR LIFE)

I do not deserve God
Who would stoop so far
And lift me up so high

I do not deserve God
Who would break His own heart
To purify one like mine

I do not deserve God
Who would open His arms
And willingly die

I do not deserve God
Who would win my heart's war
To sanctify my tortured mind

I do not deserve God
Who would revive my dying star
And be my new reason for life

Greater love hath no man than this, that a man lay down his life for his friends.

GREATER LOVE

There is no greater love,
Than the kind God gives us;
There is no greater mercy,
Given to offer us forgiveness.

There is no greater joy,
Than the hope God gives us;
There is no greater gift given,
Than the precious blood of Jesus.

There is no greater relationship,
Than the friendship God gives us;
There is no greater sacrifice,
Than the death of His Son Jesus.

There is no greater strength,
Than the faith God gives us;
There is no greater grace given,
Than His own righteousness.

There is no greater glory,
Than the life God gives us;
There is no greater love risen,
Than the eternal life of Jesus.

These things I command you, that ye love one another.

JOHN 15:13-17

GREEN PASTURES

The Lord is my Shepherd
I will always be in need
I need His protection
As I continue to believe

The Lord is my Savior
I could never save myself
I am lost without His love
In this world bent on Hell

The Lord is my Sovereign
He's in control of my life
Nothing happens outside His will
Even though we cry and wonder why

The Lord is my Strength
I will always remain weak
Only then can I really see
How my God takes care of me

The Lord is my shepherd
I shall not be in want
He makes me lie down
In green pastures
He leads me beside
Still waters*

—•●•⤳•●•—

The Lord is my Shepherd; I shall not want.
I will dwell in the house of the Lord forever.
PSALM 23:1, 6

—•●•⤳•●•—

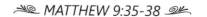

HARVEST TIME

Pray to the Lord of the Harvest,
For a faith of sincere amazement;
Pray to the Lord of the Harvest,
For a hope full of expression.

Pray to the Lord of the Harvest,
For a love of holy compassion;
Pray to the Lord of the Harvest,
For a life of peaceful enjoyment.

Pray to the Lord of the Harvest,
For a light of faithful enthusiasm;
Pray to Christ the Lord of the Harvest,
For a pure heart of joyful encouragement.

Pray to the Lord He will make you His servant,
Put your trust in the One Who rose to set us free;
The season is right for many workers to be sent,
It is clearly harvest time and the fields are ready!

HEARTBEAT OF LOVE

Listen and hear the Word of the Lord,
Hear and feel the Heartbeat of God;
Listen and learn He knows all men,
Hear and believe how much He loves you.

Watch and see the Word of the Lord,
Look and feel the Heartbeat of God;
Watch and learn He judges all men,
Look and believe how much He loves you.

Eat and taste the Word of the Lord,
Taste and feel the Heartbeat of God;
Eat and learn He fellowships with men,
Taste and believe how much He loves you.

Come and touch the Word of the Lord,
Touch and be healed by the Heartbeat of God;
Come to the Lamb slaughtered to redeem fallen men,
Feel His scars and believe in His love.

PSALM 33:6-15

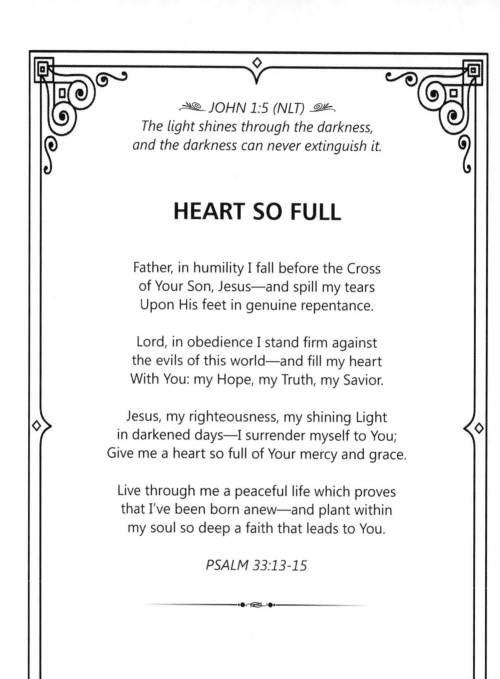

⁓ JOHN 1:5 (NLT) ⁓
The light shines through the darkness,
and the darkness can never extinguish it.

HEART SO FULL

Father, in humility I fall before the Cross
of Your Son, Jesus—and spill my tears
Upon His feet in genuine repentance.

Lord, in obedience I stand firm against
the evils of this world—and fill my heart
With You: my Hope, my Truth, my Savior.

Jesus, my righteousness, my shining Light
in darkened days—I surrender myself to You;
Give me a heart so full of Your mercy and grace.

Live through me a peaceful life which proves
that I've been born anew—and plant within
my soul so deep a faith that leads to You.

PSALM 33:13-15

HEAVEN'S LIGHT

The LIGHT stays on,
When darkness comes:
When all sight is gone,
Heaven's LIGHT is still on.

When temptation comes,
And leads you far from home;
And Satan seems to have won,
The LIGHT is still on.

The LIGHT stays on,
When the end is drawing near;
When youth is all but gone,
The LIGHT is still on.

When lies begin to overwhelm,
And turn your heart away from Jesus;
When hope in God cannot be found,
And you ask the question: What is truth?
Remember: Heaven's LIGHT stays on for you!

God is light, in Him there is no darkness.
1 John 1:5

In this was manifested the love of God toward us,
because that God sent his only begotten Son into
the world, that we might live through him.

HIS LOVE AMONG US

For God so loved the world,
He gave His one, His only Son;
To show He cared enough to die,
To save us from the Devil's lie,

If I could write a poem for you,
And share my joy in rhyme;
That poem would be for Jesus first,
Who taught us love precedes our works.

If I could share my heart with you,
And bear my soul to God our Father;
The testimony I would gladly choose,
Is the hope His Son our Lord made sure.

If I could write a song for you,
And share my heart in simple verse;
That song would be for our God first,
Who chose to show what love is worth.

If I could shine my faith for you,
And bring to light eternal truth;
The glorious event I would surely tell,
Is the one that saves our souls from Hell.

Words can never fully express,
The joy we have in Jesus;
God loves us so much He gave His very best,
And brought His Light into this world's darkness

Since Jesus gave His life for you,
And shed His blood to forgive your sins;
Won't you receive God's gift of truth,
Choose to die and live for Him?

*For God so loved the world He gave His one and only Son, that
whoever believes in Him shall not perish but have eternal life.*
JOHN 3:161

HOLD ON

Hold on, there's mercy in the morning light,

Hold on, there's peace in doing what's right;

Hold on, there's joy in living for the Lord,

Hold on to Jesus.

HEBREWS 10:36

*. . . I will come again and will take you to
myself, that where I am you may be also.*

A PLACE CALLED HOME

Guide me Spirit—lead me,
Harvest Your fruit of my heart;
Remove all blindness from me,
Create in me new eyes to see.

Hold me Jesus—protect me,
In Your truth renew my mind;
Use me for our Father's glory,
Make me a place at Your side.

Love me Father—forgive me,
Work Your mercy into my soul;
Let me learn Christ-like humility,
Save me a place at His table.

Search me God and know me,
Take control of all I call my own;
Capture me now—set me free,
Prepare for me a place called home.

Therefore the Lord himself shall give you a sign;
Behold, a virgin shall conceive, and bear a son,
and shall call his name Immanuel. ~ ISAIAH 7:14

For to us a child is born, to us a son is given, and the government will
be on his shoulders. And he will be called Wonderful Counselor, Mighty
God, Everlasting Father, Prince of Peace. ~ ISAIAH 9:6

IMMANUEL

God is with us,
He is our Living Lord;
Our Savior is Christ Jesus,
The Wonderful Counselor!

God is with us,
Conceived through the Holy Spirit;
Our Hope rests by faith in God's Son,
The Lord of Life, our Sovereign King!

God is with us,
A baby born—one day to die on a cross;
Our Salvation found in the Blood of Jesus,
Our only Righteousness, the Mighty God!

God is with us,
A Man, a Lamb, crucified to conquer sin & death forever;
We are called out of Satan's dungeon into Christ's love,
Our Resurrection Truth, and Everlasting Father!

In the hearts of those who know Jesus,
Our God is with us and always will be;
He is the Alpha & Omega, Beginning & End,
Who is, and was, and is to come, the Prince of Peace!

MATTHEW 1:21-25

IN FAITH YOU WILL STAND

IS THERE STILL ROOM IN
YOUR HEART? HAVE YOU
ASKED THE LORD JESUS
TO FILL EVERY PART?

IS THERE STILL SPACE
IN YOUR MIND? ARE YOU
LIVING YOUR LIFE THE
WAY GOD DESIGNED?

DO YOU STILL RESERVE THE
RIGHT TO YOUR OWN WAY?
DO YOU STILL WRITE THE
DICTATES OF YOUR OWN FAITH?

DO YOU STILL BELIEVE THE
WORLD REVOLVES AROUND YOU?
IS THE CENTER OF YOUR LIFE
STILL GOD'S TRUTH?

ARE THESE QUESTIONS A DRAIN
ON YOUR SPIRITUAL MAN?
THEN YOU HAVE YET TO LEARN:
IN FAITH YOU WILL STAND.

EPHESIANS 2:10
For we are his workmanship, created in Christ Jesus

INTERLUDE

Spread your wings high and fly,
Fly high and strong by faith;
Raise your voice and sing,
Choose to live again.

Turn your eyes away and obey,
Obey the Word of God;
Fold your hands and pray,
Surrender at The Cross!

Bow your heart low and submit,
Submit to the Lord of Life,
Lift your hands up and worship,
Let go of all your pride!

Come to Jesus now and believe,
Believe in the power of God;
Open your heart and receive,
Serve Him with all you've got!

IN THE LIGHT

With Jesus in my sight
I have the vision to do things right
And prove to those to whom I face
Jesus Christ, my Lord, is alive today

With Jesus in my heart
I know the way to do my part
And tell "the lost" that God does care
Enough to answer every prayer

With Jesus Christ filling my mind
I find the will to leave my pride behind
And give God my Father glory everyday
In what I think and what I say

With Christ alive and in my soul
I possess the truth Who makes lives whole
The hope I share to encourage others
Brings joy and peace to my sisters and brothers

With the love of God I live for Christ Jesus
To spread the truth of the Gospel that frees us
Standing in the presence of pure holiness
I bow my heart in the light of Thy countenance

With Jesus on my side all good things are possible
With Jesus on my side my joy remains full
With Jesus on my side I am more than a conqueror
I am a mighty warrior in the light of His Word!

Lord, lift thou up the light of thy countenance upon us.
PSALM 4:6

IN YOUR EYES

I see a rainbow of colors
A bright and beautiful vision
Warm feelings and tender emotions
Shining free from shadow's darkness

Open wide to God's clear light
Colors of joy and wonder radiate
Influencing all that surround you
Ensuring happiness

I see calm waters of true serenity
Forever flowing, soothing my spirit
Your faith touches my soul
And enriches my life

I glimpse God's own reflection in your eyes!

Dance my darling, dance!

I LOVE YOU, EVELYN
I will always love you!

THANK YOU, JESUS!

Put on the whole armour of God,
that ye may be able to stand . . .

JESUS IN MY HEART

With Jesus in my heart
I have the power to do my part;
I have the light that conquers dark
With Jesus in my heart!

With Jesus in my mind
I can humbly leave my pride behind
And give God the glory every day
In what I think and say.

With Jesus in my soul
I have the truth that makes lives whole
The hope I share with so many others
Brings joy to life in my sisters and brothers!

With Christ Jesus in this world
God's enemies may run, but they can't hide
They are cut down with the Spirit's Sword
When we wield the truth found in God's Word!

I stand fully clothed in the armor of God
And rest my case at the foot of the Cross
With the Lord Jesus Christ in my life
I am strong and victorious in His might!

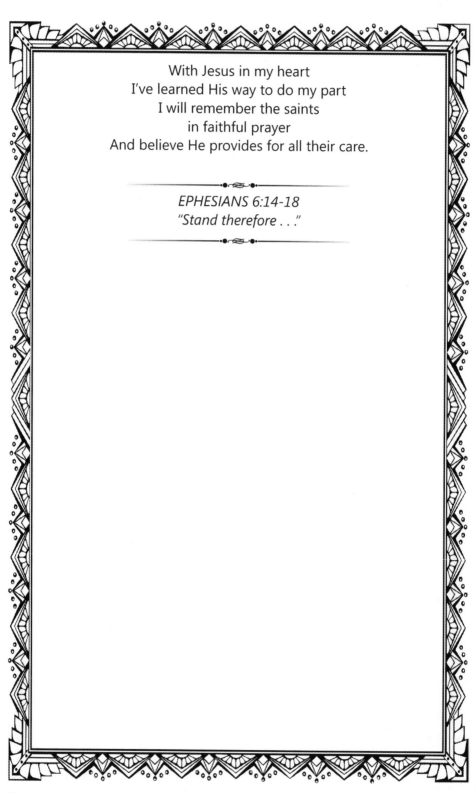

With Jesus in my heart
I've learned His way to do my part
I will remember the saints
in faithful prayer
And believe He provides for all their care.

EPHESIANS 6:14-18
"Stand therefore . . ."

JUST A LITTLE GRACE

Just a little grace
Is really all it takes
To turn a broken heart
Into a born-again smile

Just a little grace
Is all it takes
To help a suffering soul
Through a difficult trial

Just a little grace
Is really all it takes
To show a stubborn sinner
God's amazing love

To point to Jesus
And tell about His Cross
A little sovereign grace
Is more than just enough

KEEP ON!

Have you been asking God for something?
You can be sure He will answer you with what is best.
He may seal your question with a "No",
Or He may bless your query with a "Yes".

Expectant hope is second nature,
No matter how long the Lord may take.
Although you cannot predict the future,
Necessary virtue is in the wait.

Let patience do its perfect work,
As you praise God for His timing.
Trust the Lord to make a way,
In the meantime keep on rhyming!

HEBREWS 11:6

LIFT HIM UP

Lift up the name of Jesus,
He is worthy to be praised;
If you fall reach up to Him alone,
None other will carry you home.

Lift up the name of Jesus,
Take your cross and follow Him;
Discover His faith, hope, and love,
Conquers our aimless desire to sin.

Lift up the name of Jesus,
Exalt Him with your dying breath;
Live your life like there's no tomorrow,
For forever He has conquered death.

Lift up the name of Jesus,
He's not heavy – He's pure light!
He will see you through the darkness,
And be with you on the other side.

PSALM 59:10

LIGHT

*Love shone
Into the darkness
God's compassionate
Heart to overcome
The world*

JOHN 16:33

LIGHT SHINE

In this world full of fallen men,
Lift your head up and live again;
Hear the Lord calling you into His line,
Follow His lead and let your light shine!

In this world of broken hearts,
Lay your burdens down and let the
healing start; Cast your cares upon
the Lord and hear him say, "Now,
they're mine." Follow His example
and let your light shine!

In this world of token love,
Throw your treasures out and set
your sights on what's above;
Seek Gods kingdom first and His
righteousness is what you'll find,
Join in His "great commission"
and let your great light shine!

In this world of empty promises,
Put your faith in God who does
what He says; Trust Jesus Christ
is the Way, the Truth, and the Life,
Love Him with all your heart
and let your light shine!

In this world full of lifeless idols,
Sing your praises, bow your heart to
the Living God; Know Gods Word
(His Love, His Grace) is active and alive,
Share what you have and let your light shine!

"You are the light of the world."
MATTHEW 5:14-16

LIFE BY FAITH

By faith I pray in Jesus? Name
For eyes of grace to see myself as new;
That I will never ever be the same
Old man that I once knew.

By faith I pray to God, my Father
Who says that I'm akin to Abraham:
Help me rest assured at Your altar,
While I love and serve my fellow man.

By faith I lift up holy hands
Cleansed by the Blood of Jesus;
I bow my heart to His commands,
I know that it's His Word that frees us.

By faith I believe God's Word is truth,
Designed to save my soul;
I trust I'll eat enough spiritual food
To make my knowledge of Him whole.

By faith I pray with the Holy Spirit
For opportunities to share God's love
With those who won't hear of it;
'cause they don't trust "that spiritual stuff".

By faith I pray You'll break down walls
That separate us from each other.
Let Your compassion flow when those walls fall,
Into my sisters and my brothers.

By faith I walk in fellowship
With my neighbors and my God;
I will confess and repent of every sin
And enjoy this privilege as His son.

By faith I stand on every promise
Revealed to those who are God's people;
Who've found their treasure in Christ Jesus
In this cosmos of the feeble.

By faith I give up on my confusion
I surrender my foolish wisdom
As I let my Lord untie the knots
I pray for light that comes from God.

Father, I pray Your light will change me,
And color every thought I have with grace;
Help me walk in purity and live my life by faith.

~⊛ *ROMANS 8:15* ⊛~
For ye have not received the spirit of bondage again to fear; but ye have received the Spirit of adoption, whereby we cry, Abba, Father.

LIGHT OF LIFE

Once upon a time,
When light could not be found;
I stumbled through the night,
Not caring I was bound.

Back when I was falling,
Away from anything of value;
I received a mighty calling,
I knew had to be The Truth.

A New Spirit I felt lifting me,
Gave me hope to break my chains;
Before I knew it I had been set free,
And discovered Jesus is the Only Way.

Adopted as our Father's child.
All the promises of God are mine;
Purchased by the blood of Christ my Lord,
Now I walk without fear in the Light of Life.

———————•❧•———————

LISTEN TO THE TRUTH

I might not do it like you'd like,
But brother I have to tell you,
You are missing out on real life,
There is no darkness in the Truth.

I love you and you need to know,
Christ Jesus loves you so much more,
He brought light into this dying world,
And lives to be your King and Lord.

I love you and you need to hear,
Jesus Christ not only saves;
He stays with you and conquers
All your fears.

I love you and you need to understand,
Jesus doesn't just love you;
He formed you in our mother's womb,
And gave us all a will to choose.

My brother I love you today and every day,
But I hope you'll look past now and see;
Eternity awaits . . .
Only Jesus Christ can make you free.

Therefore, my beloved brethren, be ye steadfast,
unmovable, always abounding in the work of the Lord,
. . . your labor is not in vain in the Lord.

LIVE THROUGH ME

It's not enough to just be free,
Living Truth must live in me;
And be a light that always shines,
In a world so prone to hate Christ's kind.

Faith must motivate my action,
As I guard my heart against all sin;
And lend a hand to work for good,
In a world that persecutes servant hood.

Hope must be the keynote of my message,
As I proclaim the mighty Name of Jesus;
And encourage the lost with songs of life,
In this world of abortion and suicide.

Love must be the master of my soul,
As I pray that others would be made whole;
And come to know Christ Jesus as their Savior,
In this hate-filled world that crucified our Lord.

It's not enough to just be free,
Truth must also live through me!

JOHN 8:31-34
THE TRUTH SHALL SET YOU FREE

LIVE YOUR LIFE BY FAITH

In this world of broken hearts,
Fractured by our faithless falling;
Nothing else can help the divided see,
But the Truth of Christ that sets us free.

In this world of clay-pot people,
Hardened by their adventures in sin,
Nothing but the blood of Jesus Christ,
Will cleanse us from the filth we're in.

In this world of beachfront castles,
Built up on foundations of shifting sand;
Nothing keeps you safe in life's many storms,
Except the Lord who will cause you to stand.

In this world of darkness unmoved,
The Light is shown for those who will see;
Nothing will save you but Jesus who loves you,
Open your eyes and don't be deceived.

In this world where weakness is spit upon,
True Strength can be found only One Way;
Follow the Lord who chose to be humble,
Die to your self and live your life by faith.

PHILIPPIANS 4:13
I CAN DO ALL THINGS THROUGH CHRIST

LIVING HOPE

Splinters crack beneath the hand
that gave the earth its splendor,
Pain shoots up the arms and legs
through the heart in Heavens' center.

Blood spills out the savage wounds
inflicted on God's precious Son.

Our victory in Jesus Christ has only just begun!

The shock wave of man's cruelty
Has filled the earth like thunder,

But the cross on which our Lord was nailed
could not keep our Savior under.

The painful death He suffered
Was only the way of His demise,
The stone that rolled from off His tomb
is the new focus of our eyes.

He is alive forevermore! Our joy is made complete!
When you take your focus off His death
Living Hope is what you'll see!

LIVING POETRY

I've heard it said
God wakes the dead
and fills them with His Spirit,
If you WILL listen with your heart
By faith I'm sure you'll hear it.

He cuts through darkness
With the purest of LIGHT,
And makes us perfect in His sight.
Jesus knows those who are His own,
He's the One who brings us HOME.

I've heard and read God saves the dead,
and becomes their ONLY hope to live again;
When we come to the end of ourselves,
He starts a work that never ends!
God's living poetry is perfect,
His promises are not forgotten;
Things work for the good of those
for whom Our Father's Son was sent.

I've heard it said God wakes the dead,
and opens the eyes of their hearts;
Even now by faith if you trust in Him
You too will start to see.

LIVING PROOF

Jesus, Lord Jesus,
The perfect example;
His words, His walk,
An apodictic model.

God's Son become a Man,
The personification of purity;
His wisdom, His way,
A comprehensive image.

His Birth, His Life,
His Death, Resurrection,
An all-inclusive role model.
Christ Jesus, our only hope,
Our Shepherd and our Savior.

Jesus, impeccable Jesus,
Teacher, Master, sovereign Lord;
Jesus, Lord Jesus, the paradigm of power,
Living Proof of God's great love.

2 CORINTHIANS 4:7

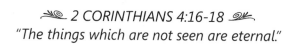

"The things which are not seen are eternal."

LOOK AGAIN

If I may enable your failing sight,
I will introduce you to JESUS CHRIST;
How God Himself loves you so very much,
He gave Himself: the Way, the Truth, the Life.

If I may encourage your sinking heart,
I will write a song of praise and worship;
How God Himself upholds the believer,
And gives them real peace in His Spirit.

If I may engage your heart and mind,
I will remind you of God's most holy love;
How He Himself sent His Son to save and sanctify us,
To be His hands and feet, living saints of salt and light.

If I may encounter the seeking soul,
I tell the Story of Christmas and the Cross;
How God Himself took the form of a tiny baby,
Lived a sinless life, died and rose to make you whole.

If I may envision the coming Lord,
I see Him HIGH and LIFTED UP;
Coming back again,
Riding on dark and stormy clouds,
To rescue us from sure destruction.

LOVE GOD

IN THE BEGINNING GOD.

IN THE CENTER GOD.

IN THE END GOD.

ROMANS 8:28

———
———
——
——
—
-

All things work together for good toward those who love God.

LOVE ONE ANOTHER

In this world of strife and pain,
Turn your heart to Christ and pray;
Pray that God will be reconciled to others,
As you share His love with sister and brother.

In this world full of grief and woe,
Choose to come to Jesus and follow;
Follow so that Christ will lead the way,
As you share with someone the life He gave.

In this world of sin and death,
Renew your mind in Christ and learn;
Learn that God will use your new knowledge,
As you share your faith with those you serve.

In this world of hate and fear,
Surrender your soul to Jesus and come nearer;
Nearer the cross where Christ died to save you from sin,
And share God's love with another in this world we're in.

1 JOHN 4:7

LOVE REFLECTION

We may walk by faith not by sight,
That doesn't mean we don't know where we're going;
We may not know exactly what Heaven looks like,
But the Light that we follow is no will-o'-the-wisp.

The way we travel is a well-worn path,
Walked by those who knew Jesus in this world we live in;
The Way of mercy and grace is free of God's wrath,
For those who know Jesus redeemed us from all sin.

This road we walk by faith is often full of frightful storms,
But we know the One who give us rest and peace;
We call Him King of Kings, Mighty God, Sovereign Lord,
When darkness closes in He is the Rock on Whom we lean.

JESUS (SAVIOR)—His God-given Name at birth,
He's the One Who opens eyes of hearts to see by faith;
The light we see at the end of our time here on earth,
Is the love of God reflecting off His glorious face!

LOVE SONG

Forever you'll be on my mind,
Forever you'll be in my heart;
Forever you'll be my pure light,
Forever you will be mine!

In your eyes I saw the Son:
The Love of God for everyone,
In your soul I found the joy
Of every treasure in Heaven.

Forever you'll be by my side,
Forever your hand will be in mine;
Forever our hearts will be as one,
Together forever in love!

PSALM 34:3
"Oh magnify the Lord with me,
and let us exalt His name together."

MAGNIFY THE LORD

Enlarge my heart, oh my Father,
Fill my mind with the joy of treasures above;
Cause me to worship, God, cause me to worship
Your Son, my Lord, who alone is worthy of my love.

Strengthen my heart, oh my Savior,
Still my anxiety in the knowledge of Your truth;
Cause me to worship, God, cause me to be thankful
For all that You are, Lord, cause me to adore only You.

Sanctify my heart, oh Holy Spirit,
Distill my lusts in the beauty of Your holiness;
Cause me to worship, God, cause me to be faithful
For everything that Jesus did is my claim to righteousness.

Satisfy my heart, dear God, oh my soul's desire,
Fulfill my devotion in the promise of Your patience;
Cause me to worship, Lord, cause me to magnify You
With all of my heart, soul and strength. Alleluia! Amen.

Holy, holy, holy, Lord God Almighty,
which was, and is, and is to come.

REVELATION 4:8

*This poem is written for all who are lost without Jesus or feel lost
in this world without someone they've loved for a long, long time;
May you and I find hope and be encouraged this Christmas.*

MAKE ROOM FOR JESUS

Make room for Jesus in your heart,
So full of the world you cannot see;
Leave a corner open for Christian art,
Soon God's truth will set you free.

Make room for Jesus in your soul,
So cluttered with religions of the world;
Invite God's holy Spirit to cleanse you now,
His grace will sweep through you like a flood.

Make room for Jesus in your mind,
So preoccupied with self you are others-blind;
Turn your attention to helping someone else for awhile,
Your vision will change as you walk in their shoes for a mile.

This Christmas make room for Jesus in your life,
So stressed by the traditions you can't enjoy God;
Consciously make Him part of your day and night,
And In faith before long you won't feel so lost.

ISAIAH 53:3-4
He is despised and rejected of men; a man of sorrows,
and acquainted with grief: and we hid as it were our faces
from him; he was despised, and we esteemed him not.
Surely he hath borne our griefs, and carried our sorrows: yet
we did esteem him stricken, smitten of God, and afflicted.

MAN OF SORROWS

The blood of Jesus fell like rain,
As the Man of Sorrows took my place;
A billion drops of pain and more,
Spilled from the heart of my dear Lord.

A Roman hammer came down on Him,
And forced steel spikes through His wrists;
To destroy vice He was crushed on a cross,
So generations to come would not be lost.

A river of red washed over the earth,
As the sinless Son of God bled into the dirt;
In His winter of agony Christ died for my sins,
But an Eternal spring was about to begin!

An ocean of tears fell out of heaven,
Drowning the sun during Christ's crucifixion;
The greatest price ever paid was given for me,
To flood my heart with love and set my soul free!

ISAIAH 53:5-6
But he was wounded for our transgressions, he was bruised for our
iniquities: the chastisement of our peace was upon him; and with
his stripes we are healed. All we like sheep have gone astray;
we have turned every one to his own way; and the Lord
hath laid on him the iniquity of us all.

Lay up for yourselves treasures in heaven.

METTLE OF MY HEART

Marvel of my heart,
Saved from death in Christ Jesus;
Who gave Himself at the very start
to save me from a life of selfishness.

Music of my heart,
Sung with joy to my Lord Jesus;
making melody and taking part
in the JOY of His righteousness.

Middle of my heart,
Focused on JESUS Christ my Lord;
growing closer as I hit the holy mark,
as a Born Again believer in His Word.

Master of my heart,
By all means the LORD Jesus Christ;
Who bought my soul from Satan's cart,
and gave me the treasure of eternal life.

Mettle of my heart,
Obedience to the TRUTH of Jesus;
standing by faith through peace and war,
I'm safe and forgiven in His perfect freedom.

PSALM 15:1-5

mettle \MET-ul\ noun
1 a : vigor and strength of spirit or temperament
b : staying quality : stamina
2 : quality of temperament or disposition

MORE THAN ENOUGH

It's enough for me to know
The Lord is my Shepherd,
It's enough for me to follow
The Word I have heard.

It's enough for me to rest
In the arms of the Almighty,
It's enough for me to find success
In the Living Truth that set me free.

It's enough for me to believe
In the sacrifice of my Savior,
It's enough for me to receive
Jesus the Messiah as my Lord.

It's enough for me to trust my soul is well
In the holy perfection of Heaven's love,
To be content with God and people
Is more than enough.

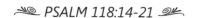

MY STRENGTH AND MY SONG

Lord Jesus, help me find my true voice,
When I come to You expressing my joy;
Oh my Lord, I want to sing about You,
With all my heart God, all of my heart!

Oh Holy Spirit, help me walk by faith,
When I cross wide paths of unfamiliar ways;
I want to hold on, help me hold on to Jesus,
With all my strength God, all of my strength!

Father, help me live to worship You,
With all of my mind; all of my soul;
While the world serves its selfish way,
Lord God, take my life, all of my life!

My Father, help me stand with true courage,
When the Liar leads me down familiar ways;
God, let me have Your hope as my confidence,
With all of Your grace, all of Your grace!

Oh Jesus, let me hear Your song,
As the world spins its hopeless lullaby;
I will love You God with all of my soul,
And remain by faith Your spotless bride!

I Love You Jesus!

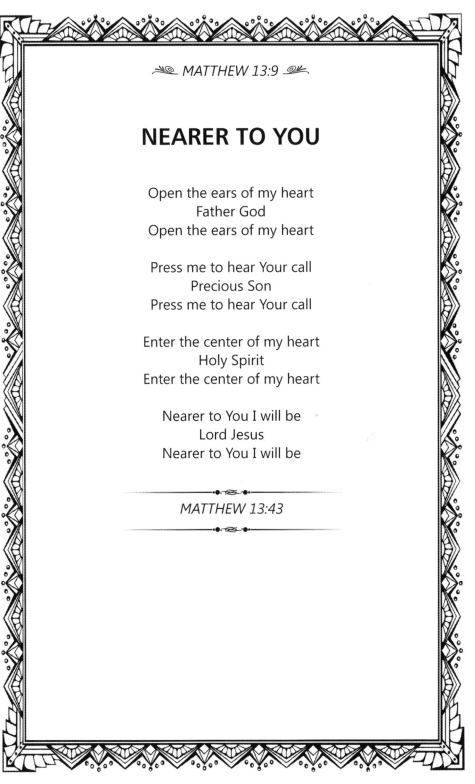

NEARER TO YOU

Open the ears of my heart
Father God
Open the ears of my heart

Press me to hear Your call
Precious Son
Press me to hear Your call

Enter the center of my heart
Holy Spirit
Enter the center of my heart

Nearer to You I will be
Lord Jesus
Nearer to You I will be

MATTHEW 13:43

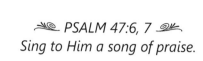
NEW SONG

I sing within this heart of mine
A song of faith for love divine,
I sing upon this rock of truth
A new song of eternal youth!

I sing inside this temple of worship
A song of praise for answered promise,
I sing about our God's faithful ways
A new song of His amazing grace!

I sing outside the walls of fear
A song of joy to soothe the ear,
I sing along this path of light
A new song found in Jesus Christ!

I sing beyond this true fellowship of the Cross
A song of glory for the grace and mercy of God,
I sing with a prayer for the lost on these lips
A new song of praise: God knows who are His!

Sing to the LORD a new song.

PSALM 98:1

ACTS 9:32-35
*And immediately he rose. And all the residents of
Lydia and Sharon saw him, and they turned to the Lord.*

NOW STRENGTH

Paralyzed by besetting sin,
I lie down depressed within;
Choosing not to stand and fight,
It is easier just to lay down and die.

Sunset comes again and steals the light,
Bringing the dreams that haunt my nights;
Believing in a Messiah I say my prayers,
Hoping Jehovah God really does care.

Stuck in this filthy bed unmade,
The Sun comes 'round for another long day;
But today the light seems warmer than before,
I heard someone say, "I am healed by the Lord!"

New strength is NOW alive inside,
I'm no longer waiting for a time to shine;
I'm standing up for all to see,
What faith in Jesus really means!

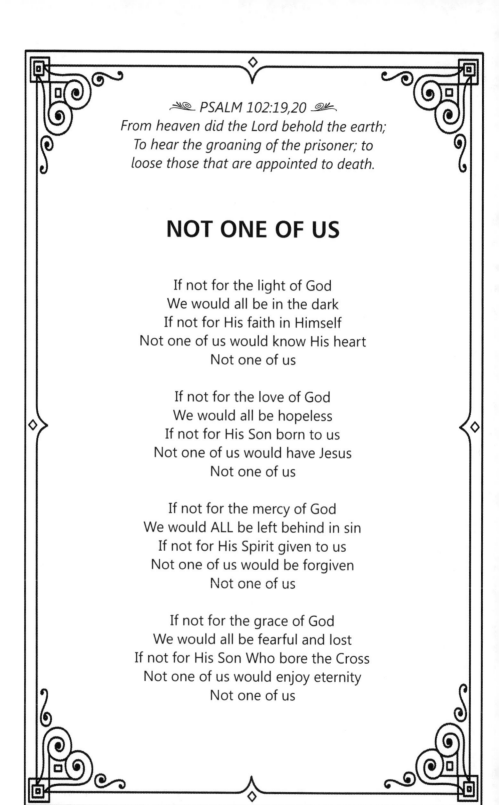

PSALM 102:19,20

From heaven did the Lord behold the earth;
To hear the groaning of the prisoner; to
loose those that are appointed to death.

NOT ONE OF US

If not for the light of God
We would all be in the dark
If not for His faith in Himself
Not one of us would know His heart
Not one of us

If not for the love of God
We would all be hopeless
If not for His Son born to us
Not one of us would have Jesus
Not one of us

If not for the mercy of God
We would ALL be left behind in sin
If not for His Spirit given to us
Not one of us would be forgiven
Not one of us

If not for the grace of God
We would all be fearful and lost
If not for His Son Who bore the Cross
Not one of us would enjoy eternity
Not one of us

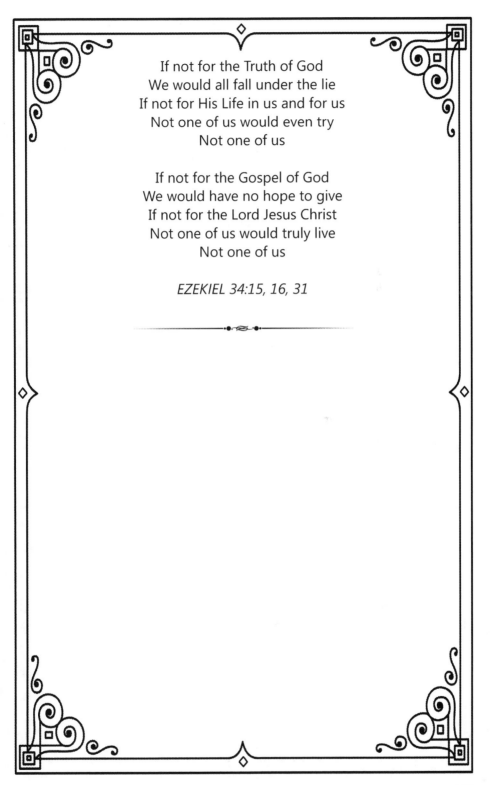

If not for the Truth of God
We would all fall under the lie
If not for His Life in us and for us
Not one of us would even try
Not one of us

If not for the Gospel of God
We would have no hope to give
If not for the Lord Jesus Christ
Not one of us would truly live
Not one of us

EZEKIEL 34:15, 16, 31

ON THE CROSS

Eye see the light of God!
Look upon this holy life
Who died for you on a cross
that you may have New Sight.

Ear hear the voice of God!
Listen to this eternal love
Who prayed for you from the cross
to His Father in Heaven Above.

Heart know the healing of God!
Learn the Truth that sets men free,
And worship God's Son who died on a cross
to give you spiritual liberty through His Victory.

Mind think the thoughts of God!
Dwell on things of everlasting worth,
but remember . . . He's no longer on that cross,
HE LIVES to satisfy all who hunger and thirst.

Soul sing the praises of God!
Find true joy by faith in Jesus Christ;
He rose from death so as you carry your cross,
you will know for certain your destination is Life!

"I am the light of the world. Whoever follows me will never walk in darkness, but will have the light of life."
JOHN 8:12 NIV

"The Atonement means that God can put me back into perfect union with Himself,
without a shadow between, through the Death of Jesus Christ."
Oswald Chambers

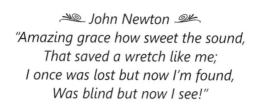

John Newton
"Amazing grace how sweet the sound,
That saved a wretch like me;
I once was lost but now I'm found,
Was blind but now I see!"

ONCE BLIND

the Holy Spirit touched me
I know this is it
my flesh quickens in His fire
this is God's Spirit
healing my desire

granting health to those bones
bringing truth to that mind
giving light to these eyes
only the faithful can see
angels all around us

rainbows on the horizon
answers to God's promises
the majesty of His Only Son
an eternal blaze of glory
the CHRISTMAS story

praise You Jesus for bearing my shame
thank you, Jesus, for loving me
love is our reward for loving Him
thank you, Lord, for taking the pain
so I could be free

dear Lord, burn a straight path
into my heart, so your righteousness
may produce devotion in me
turn my simple faith into bright light
that radiates with the power of Your glory

turn my closed mind into an open vessel
to be filled to overflowing with awesome truth
teach me to handle Your fire with fear and trembling
so others may see Your power and glorify You
Sovereign Lord, Almighty God, Blessed King!

ONE DAY

One day at a time,
One hour, one minute;
Each second is alive,
Because God is in it.

One day at a time,
New sunrise, new light;
For as long as God wills,
Every moment is life.

One day at a time,
One purpose, One plan;
Don't read between the lines,
God's Word is for every man.

One man, one woman,
Two lives are one in Christ;
With Jesus at the center,
One day at a time.

Beloved, let us love one another: for love is of God.

ONE GOD

One God
One Savior
One Hope for living

One Shield—One Sword
One perfect Holy Spirit

One Truth—One Light
One Way to The Father

One Life—One Shepherd
One King like no other

One God—One Creator
One Love that won't cease

One Mind—One Heart
One Perfect
Peace

*You will keep in perfect peace
all who trust in you,
all whose thoughts are fixed on you!*

ISAIAH 26:3 NLT

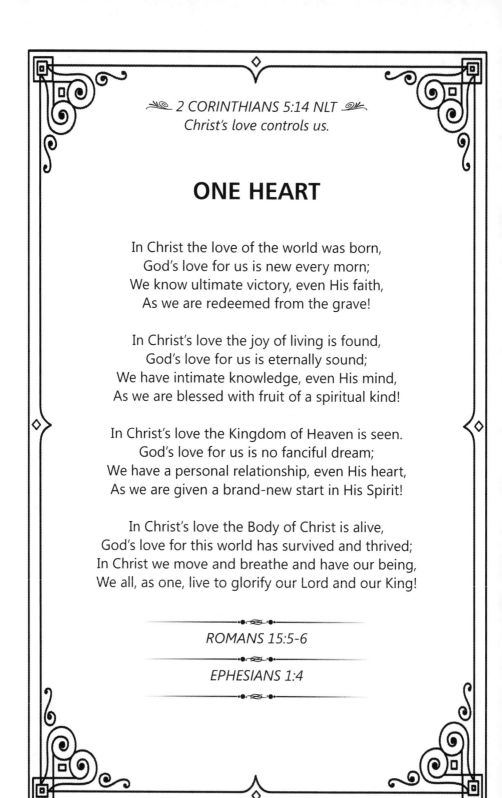

ONE HEART

In Christ the love of the world was born,
God's love for us is new every morn;
We know ultimate victory, even His faith,
As we are redeemed from the grave!

In Christ's love the joy of living is found,
God's love for us is eternally sound;
We have intimate knowledge, even His mind,
As we are blessed with fruit of a spiritual kind!

In Christ's love the Kingdom of Heaven is seen.
God's love for us is no fanciful dream;
We have a personal relationship, even His heart,
As we are given a brand-new start in His Spirit!

In Christ's love the Body of Christ is alive,
God's love for this world has survived and thrived;
In Christ we move and breathe and have our being,
We all, as one, live to glorify our Lord and our King!

ROMANS 15:5-6

EPHESIANS 1:4

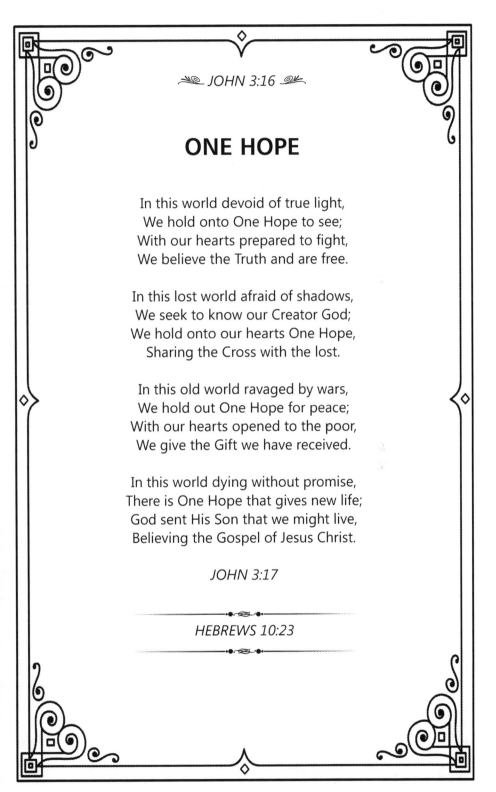

ONE HOPE

In this world devoid of true light,
We hold onto One Hope to see;
With our hearts prepared to fight,
We believe the Truth and are free.

In this lost world afraid of shadows,
We seek to know our Creator God;
We hold onto our hearts One Hope,
Sharing the Cross with the lost.

In this old world ravaged by wars,
We hold out One Hope for peace;
With our hearts opened to the poor,
We give the Gift we have received.

In this world dying without promise,
There is One Hope that gives new life;
God sent His Son that we might live,
Believing the Gospel of Jesus Christ.

JOHN 3:17

HEBREWS 10:23

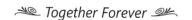 *Together Forever*

(ONE LOVE)

Forever
You'll be on my mind
Forever you'll be in my heart
Forever you'll be my pure light
Forever you'll be mine

In your eyes I saw the Son
The Love of God for everyone
In your soul I found the joy of
Every treasure in Heaven
Forever
You'll be by my side
Forever your hand will be in mine
Forever our hearts will know God's love
Together forever in love

ONE NAME

Christ and Christ alone,
He lived and died for me;
Christ and Christ alone,
His truth made me free!

Christ and Christ alone,
His love conforms my art;
Christ and Christ alone,
No other keeps my heart!

Christ and Christ alone,
Not His human mom or dad;
Christ and Christ alone,
Only Jesus makes me glad!

Christ and Christ alone,
He lives today to save my soul;
One name is worthy of praise,
Jesus Christ and Christ alone!

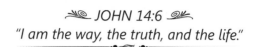

ONE TRUE GOD

One true God,
One pure Light;
One holy Spirit,
One way to Life!

Proverbs 9:10a
The fear of the Lord is the beginning of wisdom:

OUTSIDE MY WINDOW

Here in this pit of darkness I stumble,
Afraid of the light that wisdom will bring;
Telling myself its too hard to be humble,
I may never be free of this world's haunting.

Here in this slough of despair I wallow,
Afraid of the war raging inside my soul;
Hoping danger will not knock on my door,
I stay in my closet and talk to the Lord.

Here in this cave of fear I tremble,
Afraid of the world outside these walls;
Choosing safety of clouds outside my window,
I pray for the fallen who can't help but fall.

Here in this heart I hear God calling:
Turn from sin and move toward the Light.
In Christ you can help those who are falling,
Stand firm in The Faith and do what is right.

and the knowledge of the holy is understanding.

Proverbs 9:10b

---

1 JOHN 1:7
But if we walk in the light, as he is in the light, we have
fellowship one with another and the blood of Jesus Christ
His Son cleanses us from all sin.

PASS THE TORCH

Walk in the light,
as He is in the light;
Pass the torch of fellowship,
as you press onward
into Christ.

Walk in the light,
as He is in the light;
Carry the torch of hope and life,
as you march forward
through the night.

Walk in the light
as He is in the light;
Past the fire of the enemy's camp,
as you are strengthened by God
to fight the good fight.

Walk in the light
as He is in the light;
Carry the torch of faith and love,
as you march forward
through the night.

Walk in the light
as He is in the light;
Pass the torch of encouragement,
as you press onward
in Christ!

Blessed is the people that know the joyful sound:
they shall walk, O Lord, in the light of thy countenance.
Psalms 89:15

I discovered the peace of heaven early one morning looking over
John 14:27; *it*
just dawned on me that that is exactly what Jesus was leaving to comfort/console[1]
His beloved disciples when He said, "I leave you My peace. My peace I give you."

⚜ MATTHEW 16:25A ⚜
If you try to keep your life for yourself, you will lose it

PEACE OF HEAVEN

My life I surrender,
My light I extinguish,
That you would know love.

My peace I give you,
My blood I surrender,
My power I withhold,
That you will gain strength.

My peace I give you,
My heart I surrender,
My joy I relinquish,
That yours may be full.

My peace I give you,
Not as the world gives;
My peace is everlasting,
Whoever has it truly lives!

──────────●~●──────────

[1]*console vb to serve as a source of comfort to (someone) in disappointment,*
loss, sadness, etc.[from Latin consōlārī, from sōlārī to comfort; see solace]

──────────●~●──────────

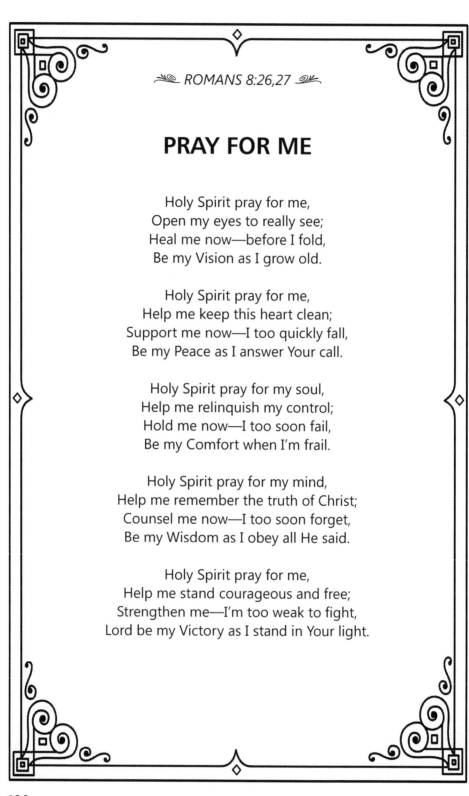

ROMANS 8:26,27

PRAY FOR ME

Holy Spirit pray for me,
Open my eyes to really see;
Heal me now—before I fold,
Be my Vision as I grow old.

Holy Spirit pray for me,
Help me keep this heart clean;
Support me now—I too quickly fall,
Be my Peace as I answer Your call.

Holy Spirit pray for my soul,
Help me relinquish my control;
Hold me now—I too soon fail,
Be my Comfort when I'm frail.

Holy Spirit pray for my mind,
Help me remember the truth of Christ;
Counsel me now—I too soon forget,
Be my Wisdom as I obey all He said.

Holy Spirit pray for me,
Help me stand courageous and free;
Strengthen me—I'm too weak to fight,
Lord be my Victory as I stand in Your light.

PRAYERFUL

Fill me Father
With Your joy,
Make me willing
To be all Yours.

Perfect the peace
You've given me;
In faith believing
I'm truly free.

Fill me Jesus
With Blood-bought hope,
Create in me
A righteous soul.

Fill me Spirit
With renewed power;
Let Your holiness transform me
This very hour.
Amen.

PUSH

Keep pressing on
Don't look back
Keep pushing forward
Follow Jesus
Out of your past

Keep hanging on
Don't give up
Keep pushing on
Follow Christ Jesus
To solid ground

Keep trusting God
Don't fall back
Keep getting up
Follow Jesus Christ
Out of the past

Keep praising God
Don't let up
Keep pressing on
Follow the Lord
On solid ground

Keep pressing on
Don't be unsure
Keep pushing forward
Follow your Lord
Into the future

Keep holding on
Don't let go
Keep pressing on
Follow your Savior
All the way home

RAINBOWS AND BUTTERFLIES (1)

I remember time before rhyme
When life had no color or joy
Then all of a sudden
An angel from heaven
Lifted me

I remember time before faith
When hope had no vision or peace
Then without warning
God gave me eyes
That could see

I remember time before Evelyn
When love had no meaning or depth
Then Jesus called
And broke down the walls
That held me

I remember time before butterflies
When rainbows meant nothing to me
When the moon was just a light in the night
And all the stars were falling

RAINBOWS AND BUTTERFLIES (2)

After Evelyn everything Is new
Life has purpose and reason is easy
Rainbows are everywhere
Butterflies are precious
And Jesus is the center of it all

After Evelyn everything is right
Light gives direction to our steps
White roses are everywhere
Ladybugs are precious
And Jesus is the center of it all

After Evelyn everything is good
Love and Peace are eternal in our home
The Truth is everywhere
The Cross is so precious
And Jesus is the center of it all

After Evelyn everything is holy pure
Laughter is genuine and encouraged
Joy is everywhere
Memories are so very precious
And Jesus is at the center of them all

I love you, Evee!
Your Jeffree

RESURRECTION CELEBRATION

It dawned on me again this morning,
As we watched for the sun to come up;
How the joy that makes our hearts sing,
Is alive because of Jesus.

Faith brought forth a joyful sound,
As we sang praise to God for life eternal;
And while cold rain poured down,
I was warmed by the words of Apostle Paul.

Although the sun itself was not seen,
The Son of God shone through the mist;
Glad hearts looking unto resurrection glory,
Was the True Light on everyone's lips.

In the joyful noise of a faithful celebration,
Let the world know you are His by choice;
And with shouts of Alleluia and Amen,
Rejoice again, again I say rejoice!

RESURRECTION LIFE!

Look up and see
What you were meant to be;
Alive in Christ,
Aware of God's sovereignty.

Look up and know
Who died to save your soul;
Believe in Christ,
Who rose from death to lead you Home.

Look up and trust
When you want no one else but Jesus;
Complete in Christ,
You will understand His Father's love.

Look up and worship
With all of your heart, soul and mind;
Dead in Christ,
We gain the power of Resurrection Life!

JOHN 11:25-26

RISEN FOR ME

Crucified for me,
My Creator did cry;
Alas, the Living Word
Gave His life for mine.

Pierced for me,
My Shepherd did bleed;
Alas, my Lord, my Savior
Laid down His life for me.

Buried for me,
The Light of my life died;
Alas, my Friend, my Brother
Was laid to rest for me.

Risen for me,
My Redeemer lives!
Alas, the Alpha—the Omega
(the Beginning and the End)
Has come back for me!

JOHN 11:25-26

RISEN

I believe;
With my mind
Open to His truth
With my heart
I follow His way
With my strength
I confess my weakness
With my spirit
I desire holy fruit
With my eyes
I long to see His face
With my soul
I claim Eternal Rest
With my faith
I believe!

You seek Jesus of Nazareth, who was crucified. He is risen! He is not here. See the place they laid Him.
Mark 16:6 [NKJV]

RISEN INDEED!

In this land of mountain and valley He is risen;
In this land of abundant provision
He is risen indeed!

In this heart of love and grief He is risen;
In this heart of trust in Jesus
He is risen indeed!

In this faith of crucifixion and death He is risen;
In this faith of resurrection and life
He is risen indeed!

In this world of the lost and found He is risen;
In His Kingdom of the chosen and redeemed
He is risen, He is risen indeed!

Inspiration: The Carpenters
"Don't worry that it's not good enough for
anyone else to hear, just sing, sing a song."

SING A SONG OF PRAISE

Sing a song of praise
With the fullness of your lungs
Sing a song of praise
To our Father's Son

Sing a song of praise
With all of your soul
Sing a song of praise to God
Who is our living hope

Sing a song of praise
With joy in your heart
Sing a song of praise
To the One who made life start

Sing a song of praise
With all of your being
Praise the Lord God who alone
Is worthy of the songs we sing

Sing a song with all your might
Even when everything seems wrong
Stand on the truth of Jesus Christ
Praise His Name! And sing a song of praise!

1 PETER 1:3

SING TO JESUS

Sing to Jesus a song of love
Lift your voices to God above
Sing to Jesus a hymn of praise
Resound the holiness of His ways

Sing to Jesus a worshipful song
Praise Him for giving His life on a cross
Sing to Jesus a new song of hope
Crowned with His righteousness
Encompassed by His grace

Sing to Jesus a song of surrender
Raise your eyes and look into His face
Sing to Jesus with His joy in your hearts
Thank Him for choosing to finish what He starts

PSALM 146:1-2

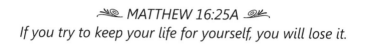

MATTHEW 16:25A
If you try to keep your life for yourself, you will lose it.

SLOW DANCE

Open your eyes
To life's pure Light
Let go of fear and worry

Plant the Truth
Grow Spiritual Fruit
Don't be in such a hurry

Give God a chance
Life is a slow dance
Full of precious memory

Hold on tight
To the One True Life
And you will not be sorry

But if you give up your life for me, you will find true life.
Matthew 16:25b (NLT)

SMALL THINGS

Even though you may be weak
you are strong in the One whom you seek
And although you are but one
you are one in a mighty army with Jesus

Even if you are labeled disabled
you can still invite others to an Eternal Table
And though you can't see how your encouragement helps
you can be of use everyday to lift up someone else

Even if your earthly horizons are lacking clear vision
Your Father in Heaven sees you through His Son Jesus
And if the work you've started here on Earth never gets done
Rest even now in the One who is the Finished Way of Salvation

Although you may be fearful and timid
don't give up on the One who loves you without limit
Keep on praising Jesus and thanking Him for your life
Nothing, not anything can separate you from God in Christ

So keep doing the small things with all of your might
and trust God in HEAVEN has a plan for EVEN your life
Get to know the Lord Jesus for Who He really is
and trust in the long run ALL THE GLORY is His

SMILE

God Loves You

Though you don't believe in God
Whether you smile or not;
God loves you sister,
Although you don't believe in God.

God knows you sister,
Though you don't know yourself;
God knows you brother,
He knows the hand that you've been dealt.

God holds you brother
In the palm of His hand
God holds you sister
In His tender command

God molds you sister
By the Spirit of the Holy One
God molds His children
Into the image of His Son

God leads you brother
Through the stormy seas of life
God leads you sister
As a humble husband does his wife

God loves you sister
He longs for you to be His own
God loves you brother
For reasons that will soon be known

God saves His children
Through faith in the Lord Jesus
God saves His children
In the only Truth Who frees us

God lives in you brother
So that we can love each other
God lives in you sister
So we can share His love with one another

God loves His children
And wants to keep us free of guilt and doubt
God loves His children
Because He knows what He's about

PHILIPPIANS 3:13,14
Forgetting those things which are behind, and reaching forth . . . I press
toward the mark for the prize of the high calling of God in Christ Jesus.

SO HIGH

The hill of the Lord,
Hand over heart I climb;
With faith in Jesus I trust,
His reason over my rhyme.

The will of the Lord,
Perfection in mind I learn;
With faith in Jesus I know,
His sovereignty directs my turn.

The joy of the Lord,
Salvation of soul I love;
With faith in Jesus I adore,
His holiness above.

The way of the Lord,
Reaching forward, upward;
With faith in Jesus I will soar,
High to Heaven's peaceful shore.

SOLDIER OF LOVE

Hold your head up,
Keep your helmet on;
Remember Jesus,
He is your salvation.

You are a soldier of love,
Marching in a world war;
Remember Jesus,
His Word is your sword.

Guard your frail human heart,
Keep your shield out in front;
Remember Jesus,
He taught you how to love.

Wrap yourself in perfect truth,
Remember: Trust in Jesus.
Let God's armor remind you,
You are a soldier of love!

EPHESIANS 6:10-18

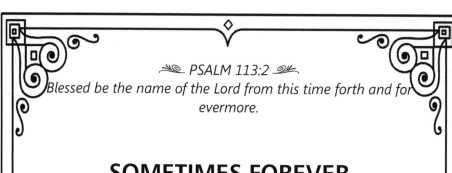

SOMETIMES FOREVER

Sometimes I get up early to be with The Lord,
Just to watch the way He creates the new day;
Sometimes I stay up late with my Lord Jesus,
And spend the night praising His mighty name.

Sometimes I sit down for hours with The King,
Just to hear the way He spoke the Living Truth;
Sometimes I kneel to worship my King Jesus,
And give Him the glory and honor He is due.

Sometimes I stand up and raise my hands to The Lamb,
Just to thank Him for rescuing my heart with His Blood;
Sometimes I'm amazed by grace when I'm with my Savior Jesus,
And I remember how He gave Himself to save those He loved.

Sometimes I'll wake up early and think about Forever,
Just to see the sunrise and think of Resurrection morn;
Sometimes I will stay up late and watch the faraway lights,
And look forward to being with Jesus at the end of time.

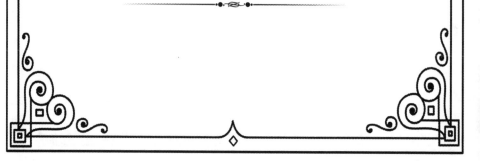

SOMEWHERE INSIDE

A little child cries
A broken spirit sighs
A heavy heart dies
A waiting soul lies

somewhere inside

A frightened child hides
A scarred spirit shuns light
A depressed heart pines
A helpless soul declines

somewhere inside

The Holy Spirit shines
A Warrior prepares to fight
A Strong Father resides
The Lord of Life reclines

somewhere inside

Love hasn't died
Faith is still alive
Hope is standing by
Truth is found in Christ

somewhere inside

Grace is holding tight

Written for a friend who was fighting for her life.

THANK YOU FATHER

SPIRIT AND PURPOSE

As one we love the Man of God
Who laid down His Life
Willingly subjecting Himself
To the Cross
Where He bled and died

As one we praise The God of man
Who rose from the grave
Sacrificially submitting Himself
So we might believe and be saved

As one we worship with hands raised
And hearts aflame
We come as one to glorify
His Holy Name.

As one we pray lovingly turning our hearts to God
Who sent His Son to prove His Love,
Dying on a man-made cross.

As one we follow Jesus accepting His victory over death;
Faithfully believing as we trace His final steps,
The Holy Spirit guides us into eternal rest.

As one we lay down our lives,
Adoring only our Lord Jesus Christ;
Openly expressing our highest desire:
To love God with all our heart, soul and mind!

PHILIPPIANS 2:1-2

STAIRWAY TO HEAVEN

For so many years
I have heard it sung
The stairway to heaven is rung by rung

I have lived long enough to learn
The only way to God is through Jesus Christ
and the Way of His Cross

Through so many tears
I have seen the steps that lead to true love
Also lead straight to Heaven

I have lived long enough
To finally understand
The stairway of love does not stand on sand

For the time I have left
I pray my faith will reach
The highest level of love that is free

2 PETER 1:5-7

He set my feet on solid ground and steadied me as I walked along.—Psalm 40:2

STAND

Stronger and stronger every day,
This walk I take in righteousness;
Always living for Christ I await,
Never nearer to God than when
Dead to sin I live by faith.

2 CORINTHIANS 5:16-21

STEADFAST LOVE

Our hope is in God's love,
God's love will bring us Home;
On strong shoulders of His grace,
We don't have to be afraid.

Our faith is in our Father,
The Father of Christ our Lord;
The Creator of Heaven and Earth,
Gave Himself to us in Jesus' Birth.

Our peace is in our Shepherd King,
The One God who reigns over everything;
Who laid down His life to be our peace,
The Savior of all who choose to believe.

Our joy is in the Lord,
The Lord of life and light;
With a holy smile on our faces,
We rest assured in His embrace.

THANK YOU GOD

Thank You God Thank You
Thank You For Your Son Our Lord
Thank You For The Sovereign Truth
Thank You God Thank You

Thank You Father Thank You
Thank You For Eternal Life
Thank You For Spiritual Fruit
Thank You God Thank You

Thank You Jesus Thank You
Thank You For Your Cross Today
Thank You For Showing Us The Way
Thank You Lord Jesus Thank You

Thank You Holy Spirit Thank You
Thank You For Compassion's Cry
Thank You For The Grace You Bring
Thank You Holy Spirit Thank You

PSALM 100:4, 5

THANKS BE TO GOD!

Thanks be to God,
For all of life and hope;
Peace to calm our restless souls,
And joy that lifts us to the heights again.

Thanks be to God,
For all of heaven and the earth;
Faith to conceive the Miracle of New Birth,
And love that binds new hearts to true friends.

Thanks be to God,
For all of truth and light;
Freedom to choose to fight the good fight,
And strength that endures to the end.

Thanks be to God,
For all of Jesus and the Way;
Contentment to carry our cross as we pray,
And grace upon grace in Christ our forgiveness. Amen!

I will give you thanks forever!

PSALM 30:11-12

THANKSGIVING TODAY

Give God thanks today,
Praise Him for His love;
Surrender to His holy Way,
Thank Him for His Son, Jesus!

Give God thanks today,
Worship Him for His mercy;
Submit to His amazing grace,
Thank Him now . . . He is worthy!

Give God thanks today,
Exalt His Name for your daily bread;
Bless the Lord with everything you say,
Thank Him for redeeming you from death!

Give God thanks today,
Magnify His holiness with your life;
Laugh, cry, sing to Him as you pray,
Thank Him today for His beautiful light!

Thanks be to God for His indescribable gift!

2 CORINTHIANS 9:15

THE CHRISTMAS CLAUSE

When Christmas Time came to Earth
at Jesus Christ our Savior's birth,
The perfect plan was set in motion
to save God's people from their sin.

The Christmas Star of Bethlehem
shone Heaven's Light on men and women,
To change the way we'd thought of God
as the Word became flesh and blood.

Lo, the Christmas Clause was added
to the eternal contract for our souls,
And faith in Jesus became the reason
the Christmas season would unfold.

So, when Christmas comes to your heart's door,
Remember you are who the Lord Jesus died for;
Celebrate your life washed in the Lamb's Blood,
And add to your Christmas gifts His undying love!

MATTHEW 1:21

THE CHRISTMAS MISSION

Born in a dark world so far from Home
From a virgin's womb to an empty tomb
The Son came to make His Father known

Born in a dirty stable outside an Inn
From baby's tears to a Roman spear
The Lamb came to take away sin

Born on a dying planet under enemy control
From Heaven's throne to a crown of thorns
The Lord and King came to save souls

Born in desperate sinners so far from hope
From the holy heart of God to a sinner's cross
THE LIGHT HAS COME TO LEAD US HOME

JOHN 3:16-21

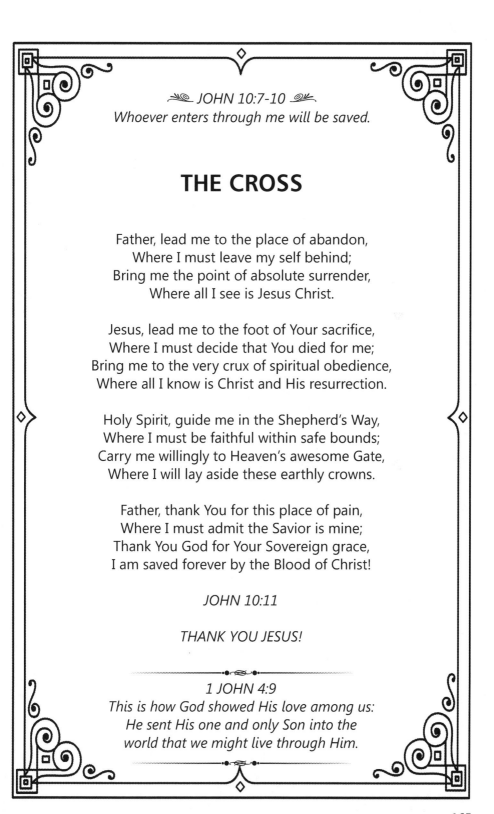

THE CROSS

Father, lead me to the place of abandon,
Where I must leave my self behind;
Bring me the point of absolute surrender,
Where all I see is Jesus Christ.

Jesus, lead me to the foot of Your sacrifice,
Where I must decide that You died for me;
Bring me to the very crux of spiritual obedience,
Where all I know is Christ and His resurrection.

Holy Spirit, guide me in the Shepherd's Way,
Where I must be faithful within safe bounds;
Carry me willingly to Heaven's awesome Gate,
Where I will lay aside these earthly crowns.

Father, thank You for this place of pain,
Where I must admit the Savior is mine;
Thank You God for Your Sovereign grace,
I am saved forever by the Blood of Christ!

JOHN 10:11

THANK YOU JESUS!

1 JOHN 4:9
This is how God showed His love among us:
He sent His one and only Son into the
world that we might live through Him.

THE CROSS OF CHRIST

On an earthen tree,
He died for me;
A Man of sorrows,
Broken and bruised.

On that same tree,
He died for you;
The God of mercy,
Beloved but abused.

On heathen ground,
He bled for me;
A Man of compassion,
Crucified and buried.

From that same ground,
He rose for me and you;
The God of forgiveness,
Holiness, love and truth.

This is love: not that we loved God,
but that He loved us and sent His Son
as an atoning sacrifice for our sins.

1 JOHN 4:10

THE FULLNESS OF CHRIST

In the fullness of Christ God's WILL will stand
Against reason or rhyme with sovereignty in hand.
His providence is secure through the best and the worst;
From the first to the last He is LORD of the universe.

King of all of Heaven enthroned in GLORY,
The Lamb of God, our only victory;
Was slain for our sin and reigns with grace;
His precious BLOOD covers our fallen race.

As we call on our Father to answer our cries
For mercies upon MERCY, no one wants to die!
Without love in our hearts still the question is WHY
Should God care for me when I don't hear and reply?

With faith in His Son Who gave us HIS all
To show us the WAY to rise when we fall,
Pressing on toward the goal shunning the darkness;
Advancing in the light of His RIGHTEOUSNESS.

Ours by proxy, a GIFT from God's Son
To those faithful few who fight and don't run.
When temptation comes testing our pride
We turn to the ONE Who rose when He died.

His WORD is our TRUTH, His BLOOD our LIFE.
His LIGHT leads the WAY in the fullness of CHRIST.

COLOSSIANS 1:24-27

THE JOY OF YOU

Hold me God in Your strong arms,
To feel the beating of Your heart;
I pray Lord I'll know You better still,
As I OBEY the whispers of Your will.

Bring me God to the Cross of choice,
To hear the thunder of Your voice;
Call me closer to Your faithful side,
And keep me FREE from Satan's lies.

Change me God into the man You desire,
As my soul conforms in Your Spirit's fire;
Teach me Father the holiness of love,
And lead me into the LIFE of Your Son.

Show me God the secret place,
To touch the contours of Your face;
Teach me God Your revealed truth,
Let me comprehend the JOY of You.

JOSHUA 1:8-9

THE LOVE HE HAS

Thank You Father for showing us how to win,
We don't have to acquiesce to compromising;
Peace for me is knowing I have all Your love,
My foundation in eternity is victory in Jesus.

Thank You Lord for sacrificing Yourself for us,
We are no longer slaves to Satan's temptations;
Freedom for me is being cleansed in Your blood,
My stronghold in heaven is the truth of Jesus.

Thank You Holy Spirit for coming to live within,
I won't pretend to lean on my strength to make it;
Life for me was crucified and rose to live again,
My joy on earth is helping others reach heaven.

Thank You God for making Yourself known to us,
I am no longer a slave to sin, I desire only Jesus;
Hope for me is Jesus interceding on my behalf,
My faith is built on believing the love He has.

JOHN 3:16-2

EPHESIANS 3:16-21

THE LOVE SONG

Established within the Heart of Love,
I pray you desire to obey and stand firm;
Together in a Christian fellowship of friends,
Remember God's love and awesome power.

Holding on to the Hope of Love,
I pray you want to grow and learn;
How wide, how high and how deep,
Are the attributes of God's character.

Aware of the Higher Call of Love,
I pray you thank our Father God;
For giving You life in Christ the Son,
Who shed His Life's Blood on the Cross.

Clothed in the Humility of Peace & Love,
I pray you realize your God-given place;
An ambassador of reconciliation toward God
Sharing the Good News of His mercy and grace.

Sanctified through the Holiness of Love,
I pray you know the full measure of God in Truth;
In His Resurrection what Jesus Christ has done,
Is finish the love song God wrote for you.

Whatever you do, whether in word or deed, do it all in the Name
of the Lord Jesus, giving thanks to God the Father through Him.

COLOSSIANS 3:12-17

THE LOVE OF GOD

We have a covering, a refuge,
The Good Shepherd from on high;
Who spoke truth, and lived truth,
And taught us how to live and die.

We have a savior, a friend,
Who took upon Himself our sin;
Who knew pain, and suffered pain,
And encouraged us to come to Him.

We have a light, an ambassador,
The King of redeemed hearts;
Who is love, and gave love,
And promised never to depart.

We have a master, a living hope,
THE LORD JESUS IS HIS NAME;
Who caused life, and causes life,
To follow Him His way.

1 JOHN 2:1-6

THE ONLY HOPE

In this old world broken by war,
We hold out one Hope for peace;
With our hearts opened to the poor,
We give The Grace we've received.

In these dark times devoid of light,
We hold onto one Hope to see;
With our hearts prepared to fight,
We believe The Truth and are free.

In this lost world afraid of shadows,
We seek to know our Creator God;
We hold onto our hearts' only Hope,
We share The Cross with the lost.

In dead lives with no promise,
Our Father is the only hope for life;
He sent His Son that we might all live,
And worship Jesus Christ.

HEBREWS 10:23

Be anxious for nothing, but in everything by prayer,
Let your thoughts be made known to God.

TRUST IN GOD

Everything you want or need
For those whom you love and care
Whatever you might beg or plead
Ask anything in grateful prayer

Whatever you might fret about
Every tall or small cause for worry
Choose instead by faith to trust in God

Talk to Him about your life
Let your Father calm your heart
You brought nothing into this world
Most surely you'll take nothing out

All that you wish or hope
Anything you have or desire
Every overarching dream
Leave it all at Jesus' feet

And the peace of God,
which surpasses all comprehension,
will guard your hearts and your minds in Christ Jesus.
PHILIPPIANS 4:7

TRUTH FOR LIFE

God of comfort
God of hope
You are Lord
Of all we know

God of counsel
God of joy
The world's trouble
We cannot avoid

God of purpose
God of grace
You are for us
Through all we face

God of glory
God of light
Your true story
Is the reason for life

2 CORINTHIANS 1:4

ECCLESIASTES 4:8

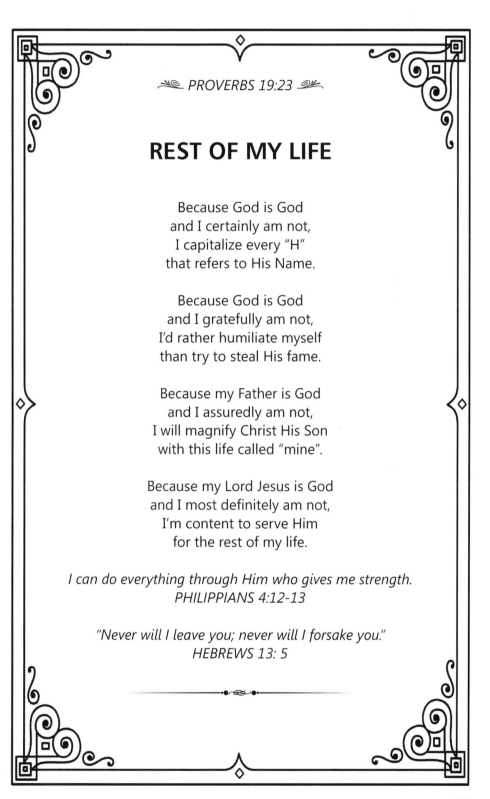

REST OF MY LIFE

Because God is God
and I certainly am not,
I capitalize every "H"
that refers to His Name.

Because God is God
and I gratefully am not,
I'd rather humiliate myself
than try to steal His fame.

Because my Father is God
and I assuredly am not,
I will magnify Christ His Son
with this life called "mine".

Because my Lord Jesus is God
and I most definitely am not,
I'm content to serve Him
for the rest of my life.

I can do everything through Him who gives me strength.
PHILIPPIANS 4:12-13

"Never will I leave you; never will I forsake you."
HEBREWS 13: 5

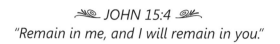

~ JOHN 15:4 ~
"Remain in me, and I will remain in you."

SAFEST PLACE

Abide in the Everlasting Vine,
Strong fruit will be found;
Abide in the Divine Life,
Your faith will be made sound.

Abide in the Glorious Light,
Your vision will become true;
Abide in your Father's sight,
His Son will always be with you.

Abide in what is good and right,
Your conscience will wear a smile;
Abide in Christ & fight the good fight,
Know victory over every trial.

Abide in the Lord Jesus Christ,
Grow up to be like Him;
Abide in the One and Only Vine,
It's the safest place to live.

"Apart from me you can do nothing."

JOHN 15:5

THE GLORY OF GOD

There will come a time—beyond rhyme,
When the children of God in Christ will shine;
And the glory of Jesus who is The First,
Will satisfy every thirst!

There will be a moment—beyond memory,
When the children of God in Christ will see;
And the glory of Jesus who alone is pure,
Will satisfy every hunger!

There will come a joy—beyond happiness,
When the children of God in Christ will rest;
And the glory of Jesus who is our hope,
Will satisfy every soul!

There will come a knowledge—beyond conscience,
When the children of God in Christ will reign;
And the grace and glory of Christ the Lamb,
Will be the Light in which we stand!

We rejoice in the hope of the glory of God!

ROMANS 5:2

THE JOY OF LETTING GO

White knuckles grabbing grace,
Hoarding love for rainy days;
Hiding seed that should be sown,
We miss the joy of letting go.

Open palms accepting grace,
Sharing love on sunny days;
Planting seed that should be sown,
We find the joy of letting go.

NUMBERS 21:8-9

God knows my heart,
Therein lies the problem:
I'd rather live in bondage to slavery,
Than look to the Cross for freedom!

THE WAY

This is a song that is written
For those the snake of death has bitten;
The way of peace keeps out Satan's poison,
The way of truth discerns all of his lies.

This is a song to be sung
For those the hornet of hell has stung.
The walk of grace begins with mercy,
The life of freedom starts with surrender.

I want You, Father, to be my King;
I want You, God Almighty, to be my everything!
Thank You, Father, for sending Your only Son;
Thank You, Jesus, for Your finished work of salvation!

This is a poem that has been rhymed,
For all those the Savior's blood has made right;
The Way of truth keeps out sin,
The Way of peace lets God's love in.

This is a poem that is prayerfully sent,
To all who know their real home is in Heaven;
If we walk in the light, as He is in the light,
The darkness of sin will be purified.

*   *   *

God knows my heart,
Therein is the blessed cure:
I believe in the atonement of Christ,
Living by faith in Jesus my mind stays pure.

PSALM 145:18-19

PSALM 43:5
O my soul?

JOHN 3:3

THERE IS HOPE

How much further will we fly?
How much farther must we run?
How many rote prayers will we say,
Till we trust in God to whom we pray?

How much higher should we climb?
How much holier must we become?
How many wasted tears will we cry,
Till we learn why Jesus came to die?

How much braver do we have to be?
How much brighter must our light become?
How many lost souls will we watch perish,
Till we choose to obey the Lord we cherish?

How much deeper shall we sink?
How much darker must the world get?
How many needless deaths will we mourn,
Till we believe there is hope when we are reborn?

'You must be born again.'—John 3:7

*Being born again, not of corruptible seed,
but of incorruptible, by the word of God,
which liveth and abideth for ever.*

1 PETER 1:23 (KJV)

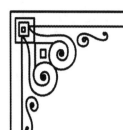

≈ MATTHEW 6:9-10 ≈
Our Father in heaven,
Hallowed be Your name.
Your kingdom come.
Your will be done
On earth as it is in heaven.

THERE MUST BE SOMEONE

There must be someone we can trust,
Outside this spinning world of slippery slopes;
A sovereign God whose heart is love,
Who is not swayed by frail human hopes.

There must be something we can believe,
Above the oppressive walls of cultural conclusions;
An omniscient God whose goal is life and peace,
Who is not surprised by faulty human indecision.

There must be somewhere we can stand,
Amidst these swirling storms of lies and doubt;
An omnipresent God whose comfort is constant,
Who is not repulsed when human weakness is found.

There must be One we can turn to,
Beyond this crumbling kingdom we call ours;
An ALMIGHTY GOD whose Word alone is Truth,
Who would rather die than leave us lost forever.

There is One whose promise is certain,
There is One who has proved God's love;
There is One who is our dearest friend,
His Name means Savior, His name is JESUS.

JOHN 6:38

"What comes into our minds when we think about God is the most important thing about us."—Chuck Swindoll

THINK OF GOD

When I think of God I see a tear

When I think of God
I see rainbows

When I think of God I see a Father

When I think of God
I see open arms

When I think of God I see a Son

When I think of God
I see a cross

When I think of God I see a smile

When I think of God
I see heaven

This is the day which the LORD has made;
Let us rejoice and be glad in it.

THIS IS THE DAY

This is the day these eyes will open,
To leave the night the light has broken;
Until I must lie down again to sleep,
Help me learn my Lord your ways to keep.

This is the day these ears will hear,
The call of God whom I love and fear;
This is the day my heart will worship,
My only Savior from death and sin.

This is the day this heart will answer,
The One whom I adore—You are my Master;
This is the day my selfishness will cease,
As my soul awakens in Your eternal release.

This is the day my soul will rejoice,
In the hope I have in Christ my Lord;
Who paid the awful price to set me free,
So I might love Him (and you) more than me.

Another day these eyes have opened,
And left behind the night light has broken;
My God, let me not lay back down to sleep,
Until I learn, my Father, Your Way to keep.

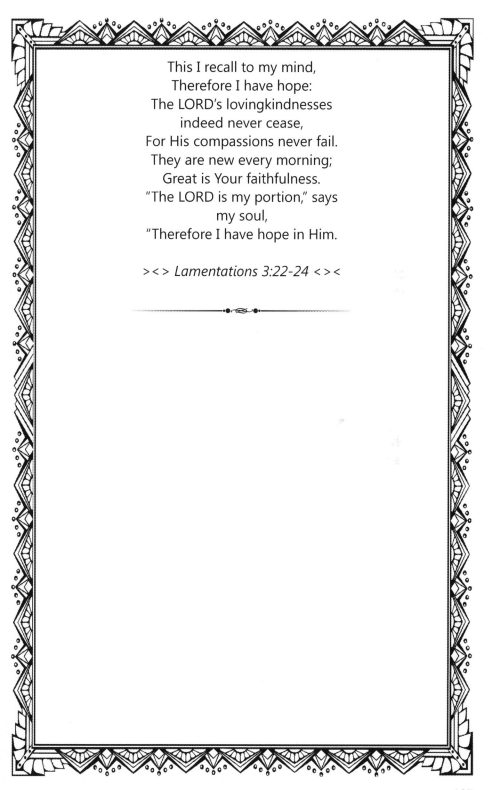

This I recall to my mind,
Therefore I have hope:
The LORD's lovingkindnesses
indeed never cease,
For His compassions never fail.
They are new every morning;
Great is Your faithfulness.
"The LORD is my portion," says
my soul,
"Therefore I have hope in Him.

> < > *Lamentations 3:22-24* < > <

TO LIVE FOR YOU

Father, Abba, Father,
Give me holy strength;
Help me fight harder,
Against sin and hate.

Jesus, Savior, Jesus,
Let me know your grace;
Hold me when I want to run,
And make my selfish getaway.

Spirit, Holy Spirit,
Stay me to the course;
Hear me when I cry for mercy,
But please consider the source.

Perfect God, Three in One,
Thank You for Your great Love;
Heal my heart and make it new,
I only want to live for You!

1 CORINTHIANS 11:1
Follow my example, as I follow the example of Christ.

TO LIVE LIKE YOU

Thank You, Jesus, for Your wisdom.
Thank You, Jesus, for Your love.
Thank You, Jesus, for Your salvation.
Thank You, Jesus, for spiritual stuff.

Thank You, Jesus, for Your holy Gospel;
The good news of it makes all things well.
Thank You, Jesus, for Your redemptive Cross;
Your sacrificial death on it attracts the lost.

Thank You, Jesus, for Your grace and mercy;
The forgiveness You give has made me free.
Thank You, Jesus, for the Spirit's fruit;
Your example shows me how to live like You.

TODAY

I will love you,
I will forgive you first;
I will hold you,
I will stay your hunger.

I will cherish you,
I will forgive your worst;
I will comfort you,
I will quench your thirst.

I will satisfy you,
I will answer all your prayers;
I will protect you,
I will save you from your fears.

I will accept you,
I will adopt you as My own;
I will receive you,
I will never leave you alone.

"Today, if you hear His voice . . ."
HEBREWS 3:15

2 CORINTHIANS 5:17
If any man be in Christ, he is a new creature: old things are passed away.

INSPIRATION: Oswald Chambers (My Utmost For His Highest)

UNCONDITIONAL SURRENDER

Look up no more,
And refuse to see:
The life you are living
Is all about Me.

Bow down no more,
And refuse to obey:
The choices you make
Are directing you My way.

Stand up no more,
And refuse to be proud:
Only strength you are given
Will raise you off the ground.

Fall down no more,
And refuse to be new:
Your discernment of your steps,
Proves you're walking in My truth.

"Let earth no more my heart divide, with Christ may I be crucified."—Wesley

UNDIVIDED

King Jesus is the epicenter of God's Word
for the redeemed hearts we have today;
We'd have no peace without a Shepherd,
Whom we will learn to follow as we pray.

The Lord Jesus is the only answer
for anxious hearts in need of rest;
We'd have no hope without a Master,
Who taught us that His Way is best.

The Lord Jesus has won first place,
in this racing heart of mine;
Mine is not to question grace,
But worship Him with all my life.

Jesus deserves our undivided attention,
in this world where blind hearts go bad;
We'd know not love if God's only Son,
Had not been sent to turn us back.

———•⇝•———

*"It is the LORD your God you must follow, and him you must revere.
Keep his commands and obey him; serve him and hold fast to him."
Deuteronomy 13:4*

———•⇝•———

*GALATIANS 2:20
"I am crucified with Christ."*

PSALM 139:16 TLB
Everyday was recorded in your Book!

ROMANS 12:1-2 NIV
Do not conform any longer to the pattern
of this world, but be transformed by the
renewing of your mind. Then you will be
able to test and approve what God's will
is—his good, pleasing and perfect will.

UNTIL THE END

In the beginning
When God was forming me
Like a poet the Potter made me
Into His own masterpiece

In the heart of God the Father
He chose to love and give me peace
And when the Creator finished His work
He wrote my name in the book of eternity

In the mind of God the Son
When Christ was transforming me
Like a poet the Redeemer saved me
Causing me to understand and believe

In the soul of God the Holy Spirit
When He agreed I would be His friend
Like a poet the Comforter held me
And holds me close until the end

*Now the Lord is the Spirit; and where the
Spirit of the Lord is, the is liberty. But
we all, with unveiled face, beholding as in
a mirror the glory of the Lord, are being
transformed into the same image from glory
to glory, just as by the Spirit of the Lord.*
2 CORINTHIANS 3:18 (NKJV)

*For we are God's masterpiece. He has created
us anew in Christ Jesus, so that we can do
the good things he planned for us long ago.*
EPHESIANS 2:10 (NLT)

UNTO THE LORD

(out of depression INTO DELIGHT)

out of the old INTO THE NEW
out of the lies INTO THE TRUTH
out of the dark INTO THE LIGHT
out of the death INTO THE LIFE

away from the world INTO HIS WORD
away from the liar UNTO THE LORD
away from the fire INTO THE FOUNTAIN
away from the valley UNTO THE MOUNTAIN

out of a life of stress and strain
INTO THE YOKE OF HIS WAY
out of night INTO THE DAY
out of chaos INTO THE PEACE

away from a divided heart UNTO THE FREE
away from the hate INTO THE LOVE
away from a discontented heart w/o hope
INTO MORE THAN ENOUGH

out of a pit of ashes
INTO THE BEAUTY OF GRACE
out of a dungeon of doubt
INTO THE POWER OF FAITH

"Behold, I am making all things new."
"Write, for these words are faithful and true."

REVELATION 21:5

UP

When life knocks you down
Look up
When pain makes you frown
Look up
The sun will still be shining
Look up
Rest in God's perfect timing

When yesterday is haunting
Look up
When tomorrow is daunting
Look up
The Son still holds your place
Look up
Live in God's grace for today

Philippians 3:8 KJV
I count all things but loss for the excellency of the knowledge of Christ Jesus my Lord.

UP TO GOD

The God of love compels my heart
Not to hide my tears inside;
"Forgiveness First" is my motto,
I know the depths of my pride.

The God of grace comforts my soul,
No effort I can hope to make
Will ever make me pure and whole,
I know the limits of my control.

The God of wisdom commands my mind,
In truth alone will I be blessed;
In surrender and obedience is my daily light,
I know the darkness all too well.

With the Almighty God in full control,
Compassion flows like Living Water;
The Way to Heaven has always been
up to God, our loving Father.

For to me, to live is Christ and to die is gain—Philippians 1:21 NIV

WALK LIKE JESUS

Take a look inside your Bible,
And find out just how Jesus lives;
Be prepared to be invaded,
By the love and tenderness He gives.

Look closely at His care and comfort,
Don't try to read between the lines;
Observe the hope He gave to others,
Despite their failings or their crimes.

Take a look at Jesus' heart,
And check His pulse of purity;
Trace the calls made to His Father,
That prayer-line is open and free.

Look mostly at His grace and mercy,
He saw everyone for who they truly were;
Study His passion and His wisdom,
You'll be amazed by what you learn.

Take a closer look at Jesus' words,
Understand His mission and His pain;
Feel the emotion of your Savior,
Realize the price He paid,

His Cross sealed your forgiveness,
Make room for Him as King and Lord;
Accept Him into your heart today,
Soon you will be with the One you adore.

WALK ON FAITH

When the enemy roars
And fear runs away
Insist on standing
True to your faith

When worries worsen
And darkness prevails
Instruct your heart
To be courageous

Stand up for Jesus
Let Him light your face
Overcome fear with love
Mercy and grace

Remember God's love
When times are darkest
Then walk on holy faith
Into God's perfect rest

PSALM 46

PSALM 19:14

WEATHER THE DAY

If every day was blue sky sunny,
And every moment full of joy;
I'd depend upon myself and money,
To satisfy this pain I know.

If I could count on every day great,
And every second perfect peace;
My prideful heart would never break,
And God would never need to speak.

If every day was darn near perfect,
And nothing could disturb my heart;
I wouldn't need an anchor or a savior,
To hold me when I fall apart.

But only God is perfect,
Only Jesus can heal my heart;
Weather the day is dry or wet,
Christ alone is light in my dark.

Wisdom is, and starts with, the humility to accept the fact
that you don't have all the right answers, and the courage
to learn to ask the right questions.—Author Unknown

WISDOM

Wisdom my friend is free for the asking,
If you are lost with no purpose for living;
Search every sage for the meaning of life,
Dabble in the darkness or dance in the light;
Only when you're willing to admit your doubt,
Might the questions you're asking help you out.

WELL-WORN PATH

I prefer the well-worn path,
The latest trends never last;
Look back in awe at the cross,
If you would worship God.

If you would approach God,
Keep your heart in good repair;
Let wisdom guard the way you walk,
If you would walk with God.

If you want to know God,
Your best bet is at the cross;
Look up in amazement at Jesus' love'
If you would know God.

If you would love God,
Watch Jesus die on an earthen cross,
Nothing else in the world was built to last,
I prefer the well-worn path.

WHEN CHRIST COMES

When Christ comes will you be ready,
Ready to meet Him in the air?
When Christ comes will you be steady,
Anchored to His heart with care?

When Christ comes will you be sure,
Sure about the salvation that is yours?
When Christ comes will you be pure,
Trusting in His righteousness, not yours?

When Christ comes will you be watching,
Watching what you say and share?
When Christ comes will you ready,
Ready to meet Him in the air?

When Christ comes will you be assured,
Prepared to meet the sovereign Lord?
Get ready now while the getting's good,
He'll be your peace in this world war.

1 THESSALONIANS 4:17

"My strength is made perfect in weakness."

WHEN I'M DOWN

How much I need the Grace of God,
To pick me up when I fall behind;
How much I need the Word of God,
To strengthen my heart & renew my mind.

How much I need the Peace of Christ,
To lift me up when my faith is small;
How much I need the Truth of Christ,
To strengthen my heart burdened by the Fall.

How much I need the Hope of Heaven,
To raise me up with Resurrection power;
How much I need the Life of Heaven,
To strengthen my heart in today's hour.

My Father, how much I need Your Spirit,
To carry me up off this heathen ground;
How much I need You, Holy Spirit,
To strengthen my heart when I'm down.

"For when I am weak, then I am strong."

2 CORINTHIANS 12:10

1 KINGS 19:12

After the earthquake a fire;
but the Lord was not in the fire:
and after the fire a still small voice.

WHISPER

I stood still and listened
As a blazing fire swept close by,
But I didn't hear the voice of God
As I watched the desert burn and die.

I stood still and listened
As the ground shook and split apart,
But I could not hear God's faithful voice
For the thunder of my racing heart.

I stood still and held on tightly
As a storm swept down upon me;
I listened for the voice of God
As I ducked and dodged flying debris.

As I stood I listened carefully
To the stillness that surrounded me,
I heard a whisper in the silence
And knew God had spoken.

"I don't require sacrifice,
The old things have passed away;
Stand still My child and bow your heart,
And you will hear My Son today.

WONDERFUL GRACE

Peace our hearts long to hold
The words of Christ are never old
Revived the dead gain life itself
Glory that won't stay on a shelf

Love only the Lord Jesus knew
The mercy of God is always new
Resounding in the songs we sing
The Light of truth dispels all sin

Holy fruit confirms our growth
The mind of Christ is ours to know
Reflecting on the Lamb of God
Our sins are nailed to His Cross!

Joy and freedom in Christ will give
God's wonderful grace the strength to live
Redeemed, reborn at His Cross of liberty
We discover JESUS CHRIST our victory!

GALATIANS 5:1

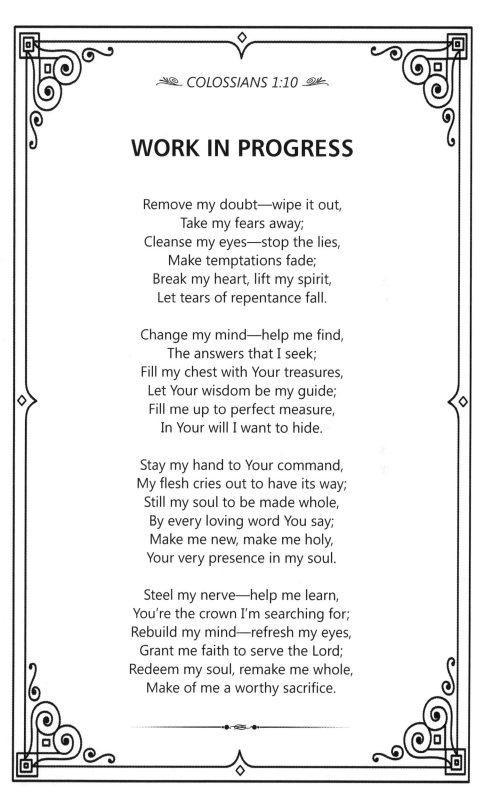

WORK IN PROGRESS

Remove my doubt—wipe it out,
Take my fears away;
Cleanse my eyes—stop the lies,
Make temptations fade;
Break my heart, lift my spirit,
Let tears of repentance fall.

Change my mind—help me find,
The answers that I seek;
Fill my chest with Your treasures,
Let Your wisdom be my guide;
Fill me up to perfect measure,
In Your will I want to hide.

Stay my hand to Your command,
My flesh cries out to have its way;
Still my soul to be made whole,
By every loving word You say;
Make me new, make me holy,
Your very presence in my soul.

Steel my nerve—help me learn,
You're the crown I'm searching for;
Rebuild my mind—refresh my eyes,
Grant me faith to serve the Lord;
Redeem my soul, remake me whole,
Make of me a worthy sacrifice.

EPHESIANS 2:8-10

WORK OF HEART

Over every Christian,
God and Father watches;
Teaching us to look to Jesus,
Helping us want to live again.

Within every Christian,
An Author and Creator lives;
Strengthening our faith in Jesus,
Renewing our minds with new motives.

Above every Christian,
A Savior and Shepherd reigns;
Directing and protecting in Jesus,
As we learn to walk in His way and obey.

Inside the heart of every Christian,
The Holy Spirit is does God's work;
Comforting and counseling in Jesus,
Those who are born again in the Lord.

For we are God's workmanship, created in Christ Jesus to do good works, which God prepared in advance for us.

ZIP—LIFE

Before you know your life is finished,
What was begun doesn't matter anymore;
When every chance you had came you do it,
You did put off till tomorrow your time to soar.

The dreams you had of what you'd accomplish,
The hopes you held of the stars you would reach;
The contentment you found in all you'd acquired,
Didn't make your world a garden of peace.

Before you know the random rush is over,
The long journey has quickly come to an end;
The decision you make to take Christ as Savior,
Guarantees soft landing when your body is dead.

Before you know every opportunity to step out in faith is gone,
The time you were given did not produce anything good or true;
But even now there's still time for you to say YES TO JESUS,
Let go of doubt before you burn out—take God's love for you!

Zip—Life flies by like a flash in the night,
Gladness or grief will be your eternal reward;
Choose today whom you will serve with your life,
As for me and my house—we will serve the Lord!

These three remain:

Faith, Hope

Love

and the greatest of these is Love.

THE JOY OF LETTING GO

With white knuckles grabbing
Hoarding love for sunny days
Hiding seed that should be sown
We miss the joy of letting go

With open palms accepting grace
Giving love on rainy days
Planting seed that should be sown
We find the joy of letting go

The *harvest*
of the earth is ripe